Mary and Archie Tisdall have had a life of travel which many would envy. Archie served in the Royal Air Force for 40 years and during this time they lived in such diverse countries as Singapore, Jordan, Libya, Tunisia and Malta.

Towards retirement they bought a motorcaravan to enable them to visit further places abroad, principally in western Europe, and gradually they began to write of their experiences for magazines.

They have travelled extensively in Spain spending many winters in the Canary Islands. This resulted, in 1984, in the publication of two guide books *Tenerife and the Western Canary Islands* and *Gran Canaria and the Eastern Canary Islands*.

Their love of Spain has taken them many times to the Balearic Islands. The outcome is a three title series on these islands — *Majorca, Menorca* and *Ibiza and Formentera*. Their sixth Travel Guide describes the beautiful island of *Madeira*, and their seventh book is *The Algarve, A Traveller's Guide*.

With the increase in the number of tourists going to Lanzarote and Fuerteventura the Eastern Canary Islands edition is now written in two separate bool͏ ͏ ͏ ͏ ͏ ͏ ͏ ͏ ͏ ͏ ͏ ͏ ͏ ͏ ͏ ͏ *Gran Canaria* and a͏ ͏ ͏ ͏r guide describing *Lanzarote*

They have two so͏ ren and when not travelling ͏

D1422331

Acknowledgements

The authors wish to thank the following people and organisations for their assistance and information, directly or indirectly, in the preparation of this book.

The Director and Staff of the Ministerio de Transportes Turismo de Gran Canaria, Cabildo Insular de Gran Canaria, including Ma. Victoria Hernandez Alvares, Patronato Insular de Turismo de Gran Canaria.

The Director and Staff of hotels and apartments, who were most helpful.

The Directors of travel agencies, especially Viajes Insular, Ultramar Express, Thomson Holidays Ltd, London, and Sharon Alexander, Brittany Ferries, Plymouth.

Grateful thanks to Yvonne Messenger, our helpful and patient editor, and our publisher Roger Lascelles and Bryn Thomas.

Finally we thank our family and friends for their practical help and encouragement.

Front cover: *Once a quiet fishing village, Puerto Rico has become a popular holiday resort, ideal for many sea sports.*

Gran Canaria

A Travel Guide

Mary and Archie Tisdall

Roger Lascelles, Cartographic and Travel Publisher
47 York Road, Brentford, Middlesex TW8 OQP. Tel: 081-847 0935

Publication Data

Title	Gran Canaria
Typeface	Phototypeset in Compugraphic Times
Photographs	The Authors
Printing	Kelso Graphics, Kelso, Scotland.
ISBN	0 903909 89 8
Edition	First 1984, This Retitled New Edition Sept 1991
Publisher	Roger Lascelles
	47 York Road, Brentford, Middlesex, TW8 0QP.
Copyright	Mary and Archie Tisdall

All rights reserved. Other than brief extracts for purposes of review no part of this publication may be produced in any form without the written consent of the publisher and copyright owner.

Distribution

Africa:	South Africa —	Faradawn, Box 17161, Hillbrow 2038
Americas:	Canada —	International Travel Maps & Books, P.O. Box 2290, Vancouver BC V6B 3W5
Asia:	India —	English Book Store, 17-L Connaught Circus/P.O. Box 328, New Delhi 110 001
	Singapore —	Graham Brash Pte Ltd., 36-C Prinsep St
Australasia:	Australia —	Rex Publications, 413 Pacific Highway, Artarmon NSW 2064. 428 3566
Europe:	Belgium —	Brussels - Peuples et Continents
	Germany —	Available through major booksellers with good foreign travel sections
	GB/Ireland —	Available through all booksellers with good foreign travel sections
	Italy —	Libreria dell'Automobile, Milano
	Netherlands —	Nilsson & Lamm BV, Weesp
	Denmark —	Copenhagen - Arnold Busck, G.E.C. Gad, Boghallen, G.E.C. Gad
	Finland —	Helsinki — Akateeminen Kirjakauppa
	Norway —	Oslo - Arne Gimnes/J.G. Tanum
	Sweden —	Stockholm/Esselte, Akademi Bokhandel, Fritzes, Hedengrens Gothenburg/Gumperts, Esselte Lund/Gleerupska
	Switzerland —	Basel/Bider: Berne/Atlas; Geneve/Artou; Lausanne/Artou: Zurich/Travel Bookshop

Contents

Part 1: Planning Your Holiday

Part 2: Island tours

Foreword

'Across the seas we beheld Seven Islands, each with its own special delight'

The aim of this guide is to inform readers about the many delights of Gran Canaria, one of the golden Canary Islands. The Canaries consist of seven main islands which lie in the Atlantic, some seventy miles (112 km) west of North Africa. They are divided into Western and Eastern Provinces, and Gran Canaria is in the Eastern Province.

With a wonderful climate all the year, sandy beaches, exotic landscapes, a range of accommodation to suit all tastes, and shops stocked with a wide selection of low priced goods, the Canary Islands are a paradise for the holidaymaker.

Details are given explaining how to get there, costs, where and when to travel, with plenty of information about accommodation, attactions and local life. Facts and information are as accurate as possible at the time of going to press. The exchange rate quoted, 194 pesetas to £1, was average at the time the book was written. These are free trade islands and you get good value for your money as many items are subject only to local taxes.

Lanzarote and Fuerteventura, the other islands of the Eastern Province, are covered in another volume of the series, as are Tenerife, La Gomera and El Hierro. We hope that these books will help you to know, visit and enjoy the Canary Islands, as we have done.

ONE

Introducing Gran Canaria

Island of Contrasts

The island of Gran Canaria is the third largest of the Canary Islands, with a population of some 550,000 and a surface area of 1532 sq km. In shape it resembles a giant pyramid, the central high mountains of Cruz de Tejeda culminating in the peak of El Pozo de la Nieves (the well of snow), 1932m. Gran Canaria offers an enormous variety of landscapes; scenery varies from high mountains with rugged peaks to large stretches of golden sands, and deep ravines *(barrancos)* divide the land, stretching inland from the coast. The north is green and cultivated but in the hot dry south only goats graze and cacti grow. This is why it is known as 'Island of Contrasts'

The capital of Gran Canaria, **Las Palmas,** is the largest urban centre in the Canary archipelago. It is from Las Palmas that the government administers the islands of Fuerteventura and Lanzarote. Las Palmas is also an international port, the most important in Spain, so it is constantly busy with cruise liners, tankers, cargo and fishing boats. It is a 'free trade' port — an added attraction for tourists.

Las Palmas is situated in the north-east of the island. Attached to it by a narrow strip of land is a tiny peninsula, **La Isleta,** now a military base and closed to the public. There are two fine sandy beaches, Playa de las Canteras on the north coastline and Playa de Alcaravaneras on the east coastline, south of the port. Hotels of international status mingle with shops large and small, with churches, monuments, parks and gardens, in this colourful, noisy city, full of life and activity.

Since it is within easy reach of Europe, Africa and the Americas, a constant flow of visitors arrive by sea and air. A regular passenger/car ferry service operating from Cadiz (Southern Spain) to Las Palmas makes the sea crossing in 48 hours. At the Aeropuerto de Gando, on the east coast 19 km from Las Palmas, jet airliners arrive frequently from London (flight time 4 hours), Madrid (less than two hours), New York (seven hours) and all over the world.

Most of the holiday hotel and villa complexes are located in the south of the island where the climate is drier. At resorts like San Agustin, Playa del Inglés and Puerto Rico, vast blocks of apartments and hotels cater for visitors. The combination of sunshine, sea and extensive golden sands provides endless pleasure and entertainment. With its spring-like climate, Gran Canaria is invigorating, giving a feeling of well-being. No need for overcoats in Gran Canaria; even on the few days when rain falls or the *sirocco* (a hot dusty wind from North Africa) blows only a lightweight windproof coat is required.

Away from the bright lights of the coastal resorts, small fishing villages provide a quieter way of life. Arguineguin and Puerto de las Nieves are two places where fish are of prime importance and you can discover little fish restaurants with an informal atmosphere. Inland towns are full of character, narrow streets have attractive typically Canarian, wooden balconies. Churches are set in cool, tree-lined squares. At Arucas the large Gothic-style church rises majestically above the town, surrounded by huge banana plantations, a sea of waving green leaves.

Gran Canaria's present landscape is the result of ancient eruptions, with canyons and gorges of rocks and lava reaching down to the sea. In the centre is Tejeda, a collapsed crater, which has three tablelands *(mesetas)*: Tamadaba, with its pine forest, and endemic botanical and ornithological species; nearby Artenara, which has cereals and pasture land; and Llanos de la Pez, from which rises the sacred Roque Nublo and where, in the sheltered canyons, the almond trees blossom. Inagua, towards the west, is a natural reserve of about four thousand hectares of wildly beautiful, rugged mountainous uplands, mostly uninhabited, which reaches down to the fertile valley of Agaete, There tropical trees, coffee bushes, mangoes and avocado flourish, while further to the south west at San Nicolás de Tolentino, in a sheltered plain, tomatoes, vines, flowers and sugar cane thrive.

In the north at Galdar and Teror palm groves and banana plantations cover the landscape. Moya, next to the deep gorge, has Los Tilos, a preserve of forty four hectares of ancient laurisilva forest. Yet another natural wonder of this 'island of contrasts' is at Firgas, where from the earth rise the famous springs, the source of bottled mineral water that is exported to all the Canary islands.

A visit must be made to the volcanic crater of La Caldera de Bandama, now covered in vegetation. From the *mirador* (viewpoint) above, there is a splendid panoramic view over the island and out to the blue Atlantic.

Perfect peace can be found in the dense forest of Pinar de Tamadaba, where the sweet smell of pines fills the air. Drive up the valley of Los Berrazales, a paradise of colour, where bougainvillea mingles with bright poinsettia growing way above the height of man. Tall palms, papaya and avocado trees and coffee create a landscape of beauty; terraced fields yield plentiful crops of potatoes, tomatoes, sweet corn and aubergines. You can hear the distant sound of bells from the goats as they climb high into the mountains. Nearby caves now updated with television aerials are still being used as dwellings by Canarians.

Situation

The Canary Islands are an archipelago of seven major islands — Tenerife, Gomera, La Palma, El Hierro, Gran Canaria, Lanzarote and Fuerteventura — and six small islets — Isla de los Lobos, Isla Graciosa, Isla de Montana Clara, Isla de Alegranza, Roque del Oeste and Roque del Este. The islands are situated in the Atlantic Ocean 112 kms west of Morocco and 1120 kms south of Spain, at a latitude of 28°. They are south of the islands of Madeira. The area of the archipelago is in the region of 7500 sq. km. The Tropic of Cancer lies 480 km to the south.

The appearance of the Canary Islands indicates that they were formed by a number of violent volcanic eruptions many years ago so there is much evidence of volcanic cones and lava. The highest point of eruption was Mount Teide, in Tenerife.

Generally speaking the five most westerly islands, Gran Canaria, Tenerife, La Palma, Gomera and El Hierro are more mountainous and green. Lanzarote and Fuerteventura being dry desert are immensely interesting and similar to parts of North Africa. The islands tend to have steep coastal cliffs in the north while the southern coasts are more level. Except for Lanzarote all have central high mountains.

The islands' features are rocky mountains, thick forests, deeply wooded ravines, fertile plains, volcanic wasteland and stretches of sand dunes. The best beaches are mainly on the east and south coasts. Some are pure golden or white, others are volcanic black sand.

Climatic Chart

Average temperature	Jan	Feb	Mar	Apr	May	Jun	Jul	Aug	Sep	Oct	Nov	Dec	Yearly
°C	17.8	17.9	18.5	19.3	20.4	22.0	23.6	24.2	24.0	23.5	21.5	18.8	21.7
°F	64.0	64.2	65.3	66.7	68.7	71.6	74.4	75.5	75.2	74.3	70.7	65.8	71
Humidity%	67	67	66	64	63	63	59	60	65	68	69	67	65
Cloudy days	2	1	0	0	1	0	0	0	0	0	1	2	7
Clear days	6	6	6	8	7	8	11	12	9	6	3	4	86
Sunny days	18	16	20	18	18	16	13	12	17	18	17	16	199
Rainy days	7.5	6	4.9	4	2	1	1	1	2	6	10	9	54

Five small islets lie off the north of Lanzarote, called Graciosa, Alegranza, Montana Clara, Roque del Oeste and Roque del Este.

The islet of Graciosa is 42 sq kms in area and can be clearly seen from Lanzarote, just a kilometre away. The population of 800 reside mainly at Caleta del Sebo, living by fishing and visits from tourists. Lovely golden beaches have been earmarked for future development. The other four islets are uninhabited, except for sea birds.

Between Lanzarote and Fuerteventura is the islet of Los Lobos, just 6.5 sq kms. The only village is El Puertito, where the fishermen supplement their income from the holidaymakers who visit from Corralejo, the port in the north of Fuerteventura. Day trips can be made only when the sea is calm. The channel between Fuerteventura and Los Lobos, called La Bocaina, is noted for its strong currents and huge Atlantic rollers. It is also a plentiful fishing ground.

Climate

The Canary Islands are warm and fresh with spring-like weather. The mean temperature varies between 25°C and 18°C, with many days of brilliant sunshine; midday temperatures can reach 32°C, or more. The average sea temperature in winter is 18°C and in summer 22°C, making all year round swimming possible.

Gran Canaria: average sea temperature, °C

January	19.04°C	July	22.16°C
February	19.32	August	22.26
March	18.74	September	23.34
April	19.02	October	22.28
May	19.68	November	23.12
June	20.94	December	20.24

(By courtesy of the Patronato de Turismo de Gran Canaria).

The small amount of rain falls mainly in the north of the islands, where it is more green with a humidity of between 60 and 69 per cent. The rainfall is governed by the mountains on each island and varies accordingly. Tenerife and Gran Canaria have more rainfall than Lanzarote and Fuerteventura. Rain is heaviest between November and February — June, July and August being the driest months.

Trasmediterranea provide a regular inter-island ferry service between all the Canary Islands.

Winds are predominantly northwesterly (*Los Alisos*) occasionally veering to easterly when they bring hot air and dusty sand from North Africa. The latter wind is called *sirocco* and usually lasts three to four days. Because of the light breezes that blow most days, the climate is invigorating and gives a sense of well being.

And because of the mountains and the fact that the islands are small land masses, there can be considerable change in the weather on the same day. The north can be cloudy while the south remains sunny. There is a saying that somewhere on every island there is sunshine every day.

The sun sinks quickly in these latitudes giving short evenings, so often spectacular sunsets are seen. The nights can be very clear and conducive to star gazing. Because of the clear air an Astro-Physical Observatory has been built on the island of La Palma.

Sufferers from bronchitis, influenza and asthma find much relief when staying in the Canary Islands, especially during the winter months. However those suffering from respiratory ailments should not settle in the city of Las Palmas, Gran Canaria, because of the acknowledged pollution problem caused by traffic congestion, dust from building projects and the occasional *sirocco* dust storm from the Sahara Desert. Sometimes even when the *sirocco* does not blow the sandy dust still comes from Africa to form a *calima*. Fortunately it rarely lasts for more than a couple of days.

During late December, January and February snow may fall on the higher mountain ranges, especially on Mount Teide in Tenerife (Spain's highest mountain) and the top of the Caldera Taburiente in the island of La Palma. In Gran Canaria, as elsewhere, the arrival of snow and rain is greatly welcomed by the locals who enjoy the relief from endless days of sunshine; it also lays the dust and encourages the growth of vegetation.

Snowfall is a signal for many in the big cities to get into their cars and brave icy roads to reach the snowline; they then have much merriment in building a large snowman on the roof of the car. This is followed by a mad dash downhill to show off to their friends on the coast where the sun is still shining.

With so little variation during the year and from one year to another, visitors can be assured of sunshine practically every day. Even if there is a cloud, it will not be cold. The few rainy days do not last for long, then the sun shines again. Thus one of the biggest incentives to visit the Canary Islands is its predictable climate.

When to go

The Canary Islands are ideal for all-the-year-round holidays. During the summer months a high proportion of Spanish nationals visit the islands. During the period October to May, the majority of visitors come from the cooler climates of Germany, Scandinavia, Holland and France. Many local shop keepers and restaurant owners take their holidays during the month of June, which (they say) can be a slack month. It is also the cheapest travel period for package tours. The peak period is from November to February when a high percentage of the accommodation is booked in advance; this is the time of the year when most tourists from the UK arrive. Christmas to New Year is the most expensive period but good value.

Because of the constant demand in the most popular tourist areas of Puerto de la Cruz in Tenerife, Playa del Inglés in Gran Canaria and Puerto del Carmen in Lanzarote, it is advisable to plan your visit in advance, especially over the Christmas period.

Some hotels and apartments have tariff variations as follows:
Low season — 1 May to 30 June; Mid season — 1 July to 31 October; High season — 1 November to 30 April

Tourist information

Visitors to the Canary Islands require a valid passport, which must be stamped by the Spanish Immigration Authority on entry, with arrival date. It is your responsibility to see this done, otherwise your entry is illegal. You do not need a visa for a stay of up to 90 days, but after this it may be necessary. Information can be obtained from: The Spanish Consulate, 20 Draycott Place, London SW3. Tel: 071 581 5921.

Up to date tourist information can be obtained from: The Spanish National Tourist Office, 57/58 St James's Street, London SW1. Tel: 071 499 0901.

Vaccinations are not normally needed for the Canary Islands. Only in the case of an epidemic would they be required.

Visitors are allowed to bring in any amount of foreign currency in notes or travellers cheques and up to 150,000 pesetas. You may take out 100,000 pesetas and foreign currency equivalent to 500,000 pesetas (£2,577).

Spanish Tourist Offices

The Spanish Tourist Industry is organised through the Secretaria de Estado, part of the Ministerio de Transportes, Turismo y Comunicaciones and funded by the State. The Secretaria has a delegation in the capital of each province and public information offices are also there.

Oficinas Municipales de Turismo are situated in towns and villages of particular tourist interest and are there to provide information, free of charge. It is recommended that use be made of these tourist offices in the Canary Islands; they can supply lists of accommodation, island and town maps, literature often with good pictures. Although in some offices the staff only have a limited knowledge of English, much effort is made to assist tourists. They can be found in:

Western Province
Tenerife: Palacio Insular, Santa Cruz de Tenerife. Tel: 24 22 27.
La Palma: Calle O'Daly, Santa Cruz de la Palma.
Gomera: Ayuntamiento, General Franco 20, San Sebastián.
El Hierro: — Cabildo Insular del Hierro, Valverde.

Eastern Province

Gran Canaria: Parque Santa Catalina, Las Palmas. Tel: 26 46 23.
Lanzarote: Parque Municipale, Arrecife.
Fuerteventura: Ministerio de Trabajo, Avenida General Franco, Puerto del Rosario.

Places of special interest in Gran Canaria

Approximate distances are given from Las Palmas (capital)

Agaete 37 kms   Picturesque small town in fertile countryside of north west.

Arguineguin 66 km   Fishing village in the south; tourists, harbour, restaurants, bars, petrol, repairs, weekly market. Apartments and hostal. Small beach.

Artenara 49 km   Highest village and one of the oldest, with people still living in cave houses. Shrine to La Virgen de la Cuevita carved out of rock, Meson Silla interesting restaurant.

Arucas 17 km   Centre of banana growing area; large town with imposing parish church, municipal park and gardens. Nearby Montana de Arucas, a volcanic cone, is good viewing point for coastline panorama.

Caldera Bandama 48 km   Spectacularly deep volcano crater 609 m above sea level, now green and peaceful. Nearby view point and golf course.

Fataga 60 km   Attractive tiny village in valley between mountains on southern route from Tejeda. Palm trees, small bars, souvenirs, shops.

Firgas 20 km   Noted for its natural spring waters that are exported to all the Canary Islands. Scenic countryside.

Galdar 40 km   Old Guanche town, now commercial centre. Town hall interesting, Guanche relics, dragon tree. Nearby cave Cueva Pintada has geometric wall paintings.

Guía 24 km   Santa Maria de Guía, the town's most important church, was first built in 1491. Guía is the birth place of José Lujan Pérez, the eighteenth century sculptor, and you can see some of his work in the church. The town is noted for its cheese *(queso de flor)* and annual cheese festival.

Ingenio 27 km   Eastern inland town, narrow streets, old houses. School of Needlework and Embroidery.

Jardín Canario 38 km   Botanical gardens in beautiful green Angostura Valley. Free entrance.

Las Palmas Capital city, important large docks, many historic buildings: Casa de Colon, Columbus House, Cathedral. Big stores and many small shops with goods from all over the world. Great variety of cafés, bars, restaurants and hotels. Lively.

Los Berrazales 57 km In Agaete, lush vegetation, high green mountains, very scenic route 6 km of exotic flowers, shrubs and trees. Restaurant.

Maspalomas 60 km One of the most beautiful beaches 7 km long. Sand dunes, swimming, bars, hotels, apartments, souvenir shopping, camel rides, fishing, golf, old lighthouse.

Pinar de Tamadaba 66 km Gran Canaria's last primeval forest in the north west at 1300 m. Canary Fir trees more than 98ft/30 m. A good road leads via Cruz de Tejeda to the heart of the forest, be careful not to get lost in the dense woodland.

Playa del Inglés 54 km The beach is over two and a half kilometres long and joins the Maspalomas sand dunes. Swimming, layout chairs, sun umbrellas, promenade. Restaurants, bars, hotels, apartments, bungalows, commercial centres, nightclubs, discos, entertainments, bright lights. Cheerful holiday resort, fun for all the family.

Puerto de Las Nieves 43 km Fishing village on west coast, two pebble beaches, swimming, fishing, Fish restaurants, souvenir shops.

Puerto Mogán 85 km Quiet fishing port in southwest. Fish restaurant, petrol, tropical fruits, local vegetables. Nine kilometres up scenic valley to village of Mogán in mountains, lush vegetation, restaurant, shops.

Puerto Rico 71 km Man-made holiday resort in southwest, good sandy beaches, two harbours, yacht marinas, pleasure and fishing boats, deep sea sport fishing. Sea excursions, water sports, tennis, bowling. Many bars, restaurants, supermarkets. Tourist entertainment. Apartments, post office, banks. Popular place with good sunshine record.

San Bartolomé de Tirajana 53 km Small pretty town at foot of mountains, palm trees, attractive houses, restaurant, views.

San Mateo 21 km Inland town, popular stopping place en route to Cruz de Tejeda. Old farmhouse museum, restaurants, Sunday market with livestock.

Santa Lucia 45 km Pleasant village on side of mountain, peaceful scenery, Guanche Museum and restaurant.

Tejeda 44 km Pretty little village, rural setting, almond and orange trees, petrol. Cruz de Tejeda is centre of island, panoramic views, bars, restaurant, souvenirs, donkey rides. National Parador.

Telde 14 km   Busy commercial town, south of Las Palmas. Good market and interesting church.

Teror 21 km   Set high in the mountains, a quiet Canary town with typical carved pine balconies. Old Canarian mansion open to the public. Seventeenth century church. Hand-made lace.

Beaches

Gran Canaria has some wonderful beaches, some of them very long. Here are some which you will surely want to visit.

Playa de las Canteras Las Palmas. Four kilometres of fine golden sands that are kept clean. Deck chairs, sun umbrellas, life guards, safe swimming.

Playa del Inglés A wonderful stretch of golden sands and shallow water, ideal for family swimming. Lifeguards.

Playa de Maspalomas Seven kilometres of marvellous golden sand and sand dunes, can be windy. Ideal for nude sun bathing. Deck chairs, sun umbrellas, beach cafés.

Playa de Melonares At present still undeveloped, a small sand and rock beach but the sea can be rough. Life guards and a small fish restaurant.

Playa Puerto Rico Busy horseshoe bay with stretch of golden sands. Crowded in high season, safe for children. Many bars, restaurants and water sports.

Playa de San Agustin A pleasant manmade beach with sand and good swimming, promenade walk.

Playa de Tauro Small bay with pebble and sand beach. Can have an undertow when windy.

The golden beach at Playa de las Canteras — viewed here from the Melia Las Palmas Hotel.

TWO

Getting there

Arrival by air

Scheduled air services from London Heathrow and Gatwick direct to the Canary Island (including Lanzarote and Fuerteventura) are provided by Iberia, the Spanish national airline, and Britannia Airways. The (current) return fare ranges widely between £129 and £250, with weekly and seasonal variations. The flight time between London/Gatwick and Las Palmas is four hours. Iberia also fly from London Heathrow to the Canaries via Madrid and Seville.

There are several charter flights used by package operators, which fly direct between the UK and the Canary Islands. Seats on these aircraft are sometimes available, without accommodation. Travel agents are able to supply details. Prices vary according to the season but can be lower than those of Iberia.

Gando airport

Gando airport, also known as **Aeropuerto de Gran Canaria,** is a two-storey building where arrivals are on the ground floor, departures on the first floor and the restaurant and viewing terrace on the second floor, which is reached by a lift. There are cafeterias and bars on all floors, and on the second floor a small shop has Canarian souvenirs. There is a duty-free shop and bar in the departure lounge. Plenty of luggage trolleys can be found on the ground and first floors, which are connected by escalators for passengers (but not trolleys). There are adequate toilet facilities including those for the disabled. A useful signposted Meeting Point is on the ground floor, and there is also a money exchange machine *(cajero automatico)* here, where one thousand peseta notes can be changed into coins for telephones, etc. There are also self-drive car hire and travel agent desks and Iberia Information. Parking, taxi rank and the bus to Las Palmas are outside.

The airport is rather austere and does not have many facilities for waiting passengers such as one finds in other international airports.

Inter island flights

Of the seven islands, La Gomera is the only one that does not have an airport but there is a project to build one near Santiago in the south of the island. There are frequent ferries from Los Cristianos in the south of Tenerife to San Sebastian de la Gomera, for those who are 'island hopping'.

Other airports in the Canaries are:

Tenerife	— Aerpuerto Los Rodeos (Inter Island)
	— Aeropuerto Reina Sofia (International)
Fuerteventura	— Aeropuerto Los Estancas (Puerto del Rosario)
Lanzarote	— Aeropuerto de Lanzarote (Arrecife)
El Hierro	— Aeropuerto del Hierro (Valverde)
La Palma	— Aeropuerto de la Palma

Note that the airport at El Hierro is virtually a landing strip, but it is of good size and sufficient for return flights each day between Tenerife and El Hierro.

On all the other islands the airports are modern and efficient and well able to cope with the traffic, which sometimes is very heavy.

The system for handling passengers and their luggage is the same as for all international airports and the Spanish have no wish to slow the flow of tourists. It is necessary only to have your passport to hand. The airports are well served with taxi and buses. Booking arrangements for hotels, apartments and car rental at Tenerife and Lanzarote can be made from the airport. At present the airport at Fuerteventura does not have the facility to book accommodation. You would need to seek the assistance of a taxi driver or travel agent *(viaje)*.

Inter island flight times and costs are as follows:

Gando Airport	to Reina Sophia/Los Rodeos	
Las Palmas	(Tenerife)	— 35 mins
(Gran Canaria)	to Los Estancos	
	(Fuerteventura)	— 30 mins
	to La Palma	
	(La Palma)	— 40 mins
	to Arrecife	
	(Lanzarote)	— 35 mins

Fares between Las Palmas and Tenerife cost 5,900 pesetas (£30.40) return; between Las Palmas and Lanzarote or Fuerteventura, 9,000 pesetas (£46.39) return; between Lanzarote and Fuerteventura, 3,600 pesetas (£18.66) return.

Arrival by sea

The only car and passenger service operating from Spain to the Canary Islands is from Cadiz (southern Spain) to Tenerife, Gran Canaria and Lanzarote, and it is operated by the Trasmediterranea Shipping Company. It is not possible to go directly to the other islands, though there are ferries to La Palma, El Hierro and Gomera from Tenerife, and to Lanzarote and Fuerteventura from Gran Canaria. But first you have to get to Cadiz . . .

By rail to Cadiz
Rail tickets for travel from UK to Cadiz, Spain, can be obtained from: **British Rail Continental Ltd** (Ticket and Information Office) P.O. Box No. 29, London SW1V 1JX, tel: 071 834 2345 or through a Travel Agent. There are no Spanish Railway Agents in UK. Typical fares: London to Cadiz, Second Class Return — £175.

By road to Cadiz
The most direct way is to cross from Plymouth (Devon) to Santander in northern Spain and then drive south to Cadiz (see section Driving in Spain, Chapter 4).

Brittany Ferries operate a regular car and passenger ferry (from Millbay Docks, Plymouth) throughout the year. The crossing takes twenty-four hours in fully stabilised ships. Driving into the car deck is a simple operation. The ships are comfortable with air-conditioned de luxe, two- and four-berth cabins, some with showers and toilets. There are wide promenade and sun decks, lounges with bars and dance floor, restaurant, duty free shop, cinema, games and children's room.

Arriving in Santander, there are many routes across Spain, the most direct being via Burgos, Madrid, Cordoba and Sevilla to Cadiz. Distance on this route is 1165 km.

One can cross to France by using any of the Channel ports and travel overland to Spain, thence down to Cadiz in the south. However, during the winter months the mountain passes in northern Spain and Andorra can be closed by snow. An alternative route is to drive down to the French Mediterranean and continue along the east coast line of Spain to reach Cadiz.

Yet another variation is to reach Spain and drive along the north east coast, then down the western coast into Portugal and along the Algarve to Spain and Cadiz. The latter route, though much longer, gives a very scenic drive.

Examples of ferry costs for a car and two persons, single, mid season are:

Plymouth to Santander — £250

Plymouth to Roscoff — £95

Portsmouth to St Malo — £126

Portsmouth to Caen — £87 (day)

Note that costs will vary with type of accommodation and length of vehicle. Further information from **Brittany Ferries,** Millbay Docks, Plymouth, P07 8RU. Tel: 0752 21321. Other channel ferries are: **P. & O. Ferries,** Freepost, Southampton, SO 91 BG; **Sealink Stena Line,** Charter House, Park Street, Ashford, Kent TN24 8EX. Tel: 0233 647047.

The ferry from Cadiz

Trasmediterranea run during the winter months one ferry a week between Cadiz (in southern Spain) and the Canary Islands. During the summer (2 June to 6 October) it crosses twice weekly. The ferry calls at Santa Cruz de Tenerife, Las Palmas de Gran Canaria and Lanzarote on every voyage, taking nearly two days to get there. This is the only ferry service operating between the Spanish peninsula and the Canaries. It is advisable to book well in advance.

There are two ferry ships operating the service at present, the 'J.J. Sister' and the 'Manuel Soto'. They are similar, of about 10,000 tons each carrying 743 passengers and 250 vehicles. Described as floating hotels, they have a swimming pool, à la carte restaurant, self-service cafeteria, bars, sport facilities, reading room, dance floor, cinema, television, shop, hairdresser, children's playroom and lifts. First and Tourist Class, two, three and four berth cabin accommodation is provided.

The Trasmediterranea ferry ships operating between the islands are smaller but services are adequate considering that the voyages are of shorter duration, about seven hours and usually overnight. First and Tourist Class accommodation is provided. All Trasmediterranea ferries have vehicle space, which is drive-on/drive-off. On occasions it may be necessary to reverse on to the car deck.

Trasmediterranea are planning to add another ship to their service between Cadiz and the Canaries. The 'Bolero', presently owned by

Fred Olsen, can carry 1600 passengers, 400 vehicles and has 748 cabins.

The UK agent for Trasmediterranea is: **Melia Travel,** 12 Dover Street, London W1. Tel: 071 499 6731. Reservations can also be made in Spain through travel agents. Trasmediterranea have offices in a number of towns in Spain.

In Cadiz: Avenida de Carranza, 26. Tel: 28 43 50. Telex 76028.
In Madrid: (Head Office) Plaza Manuel Gomez Moreno. Tel: 456 00 07. Telex 27731.
In Las Palmas: Muelle Santa Catalina. Tel: 26 00 70.
In Santa Cruz de Tenerife: Marina 59. Tel: 28 78 50.

Inter island ferry services

The Trasmediterranea Shipping Company

Trasmediterranea operates an inter island vehicle and passenger service that connects all seven islands. There is a daily service between Gran Canaria and Tenerife. The other islands of Lanzarote, Fuerteventura, Gomera, Hierro, and La Palma are visited at least twice a week. The main ports of the Canary Islands are:

Gran Canaria: Las Palmas de Gran Canaria.
Lanzarote: Arrecife, Playa Blanca.
Fuerteventura: Puerto del Rosario, Corralejo, Morro Jable, Gran Tarajal.
Tenerife: Santa Cruz de Tenerife, Los Cristianos.
La Gomera: San Sebastián de Gomera.
El Hierro: Puerto de La Estaca.
La Palma: Santa Cruz de la Palma.

The inter island ferries are usually pleasant sea crossings, despite the fact that the ships are old. In winter, owing to Atlantic squalls, the sea can be rough. There are cabins or armchairs *(butacas),* bar, cafeteria and shop available. Sailings are usually overnight. The single fare for two persons and car between Las Palmas, Gran Canaria and Lanzarote or Fuerteventura is about 20,000 pesetas (£103). Reservations can be made at most travel agents. Trasmediterranea have offices at all ports.

In addition to the vehicle and passenger ferry, Trasmediterranea operate the following Jetfoil services between:
● Las Palmas (Gran Canaria) and Santa Cruz de Tenerife, four times daily, taking 80 minutes, single fare 4220 pesetas (£21.75).

The jetfoil provides a quick way to travel between the islands.

● Santa Cruz de Tenerife and Morro Jable (Fuerteventura), once a day, taking 2 hrs, single fare, 6080 pesetas (£31.34).
● Las Palmas (Gran Canaria) and Morro Jable (Fuerteventura), once a day, taking 90 minutes, fare 4,220 pesetas (£21.75).
● Playa Blanca (Lanzarote) and Corralejo (Fuerteventura) four times daily, taking twenty minutes, single fare 1,950 pesetas (£10).
● Playa Blanca (Lanzarote) and Puerto del Rosario (Fuerteventura) taking 60 minutes, single fare 2,950 pesetas (£15.20).
● Puerto del Rosario and Corralejo (Fuerteventura), taking 40 minutes, single fare 1,000 pesetas (£5).

The Alisur Vehicle and Passenger Ferry
The Alisur Ferry Company provides six services daily between Corralejo (Fuerteventura) and Playa Blanca (Lanzarote) taking 45 minutes. It is a small open decked vessel. Single fare, 1,500 pesetas (£7.73). Vehicle and two passengers 5,500 pesetas (£28).

Ferry Betancuria
The Ferry Betancuria is a modern vehicle and passenger ferry providing a thrice daily service between Corralejo and Playa Blanca,

taking 35 minutes to make the crossing. Single fare, 2,900 pesetas (£14.94). Vehicle and two passengers, 6,900 pesetas (£35.56).

Cruises

The following companies operate inclusive luxury liner cruises to the Canary Islands:

Fred Olsen Line, 11 Conduit Street, London. Tel: 071 409 2019.

P & O 'Princess' and 'Canberra' Cruises, Beaufort House, St Botolph Street, London EC3. Tel: 071 377 2551.

Costa Cruises, Costa Line, 16 Maddox Street, London.

CTC Lines, 1 Lower Regent Street, London W1. Tel: 071 930 5833

Cunard, 8 Berkeley Street, London. Tel: 071 491 3930.

Cruise ships call at Santa Cruz de Tenerife, Las Palmas de Gran Canaria, Arrecife, Lanzarote and Santa Cruz de la Palma.

Check with your local travel agents for further details of all cruises to the Canary Islands.

Arrival by yacht

For those who have the necessary skills and a suitable yacht, it is possible to reach the Canary Islands, though it is well to realise they are in the Atlantic Ocean, not the Mediterranean. For up to date details write to:

National Assembly of Yacht Captains, Muelle España, Zona Deportiva, Barcelona, Spain; or

The Spanish Sailing Federation, Juan Vigon 23, Madrid, Spain.

Yacht and boat facilities

The Canary Islands are ideally situated for yachts and motor vessels, having many suitable marinas and moorings, natural sheltered bays and harbours. Many boats moor there for the winter season, some waiting, as Christopher Colombus did, for the trade winds to take them to the West Indies. There are yacht marinas

● In Gran Canaria:

Real Club Náutico de Gran Canaria Puerto de la Luz, Las Palmas. Tel: 24 66 90.

Puerto Deportivo de Las Palmas Puerto de La Luz, Las Palmas. Tel: 23 45 66. Facilities include, 300 moorings, 40 anchorings, fuel, water, electricity, telephone, dry dock and repair shop.

Puerto Deportivo Puerto Rico Tel: 26 48 30. Facilities include, 578 moorings (no anchoring), fuel, water, telephone, dry dock and repair shop.
Club de Yates Pasito Blanco. Tel: 76 22 59. Facilities include, 500 moorings, receiving zone, fuel, water, electricity, telephone, dry rock and repair shop.
Club Deportivo Puerto Mogan. Tel: 74 02 22. Moorings, Water, Electricity.

● In Lanzarote
Casino Club Náutico de Arrecife Arrecife. Tel: 81 18 50. Facilities include 22 moorings.
Urbanisation y Puerto Deportivo Puerto Calero. Tel: 82 55 94.
Yacht Marina Playa Blanca.

● In Fuerteventura
Puerto Deportivo, Caleta de Fuste. Tel: 87 81 01. Facilities include 150 moorings, fuel and water.
The facilities at Corralejo and Morro Jable are not yet completed.

● In Tenerife
Real Club Náutico, Carretera de San Andres, Santa Cruz de Tenerife. Tel: 27 37 00.
Puerto Deportivo Los Gigantes. Tel: 86 71 01. Facilities include, 355 moorings, fuel, water, electricity, repairs.
Puerto Pesquero Los Cristianos. Tel: 79 11 63. Facilities include fuel, water and repairs.
Club Náutico La Galera Tel: 50 09 17. Facilities include 15 moorings, fuel, water and repairs.
Puerto Deportivo Radazul Tel: 61 54 58. Facilities include, 200 moorings, fuel, water, electricity and repairs.

● In La Palma
Real Club de Santa Cruz de la Palma Tel: 41 10 78. Facilities include anchorings, fuel and water.

● In La Gomera
Club Náutico de La Gomera San Sebastián. Tel: 87 10 02. Facilities include, 22 moorings, fuel, water and repairs.

THREE

Where to stay

The range of accommodation

Accommodation in the Canaries ranges from luxury hotels to simple guesthouses and camping. In Tenerife and Gran Canaria the choice is vast. Lanzarote has increased the number of beds available to tourists recently, but the development is being strictly controlled to suit the island's amenities. Fuerteventura has a new building programme in the south. La Palma, La Gomera and El Hierro have little tourist accommodation, except for the *paradors* there.

An up to date list of all types of accommodation currently available can be obtained from the Tourist Offices. For Gran Canaria, Lanzarote and Fuerteventura write to The Tourist Office, Parque Santa Catalina, Las Palmas de Gran Canaria. Tel: 26 46 23. For Tenerife, La Palma, Gomera and El Hierro the address is: The Tourist Office (Palacio Insular), Plaza España, Santa Cruz de Tenerife. Tel: 24 22 27.

It is recommended that you choose accommodation that has been inspected by the Tourist Board and that you book through property or travel agents. It is unwise to seek unlisted places, especially in the cities where some proprietors may not observe security regulations nor maintain hygiene standards.

The cost of non package accommodation is similar on all the islands, but in each group there is a variation of tariff according to the season: high season is 1 November to 30 April; mid season is 1 July to 31 October; low season is 1 May to 30 June.

Charges range as follows for a double or twin-bedded room (without breakfast).

Five-star hotel, from 15,000 pesetas (£77.31)
Four-star hotel, from 7,000 pesetas (£36)
Three-star hotel, from 5000 pesetas (£25.77)
Two-star hotel, from 2,500 pesetas (£12.88)

One-star hotel, 2,000 pesetas (£10.30)
Pension, from 800 pesetas (£4.12)

We wish to emphasise that prices are increasing all the time and that a tax (ITE) of 4 per cent is added to all accommodation accounts.

Hotels

Hotels (*Hoteles* — H) are classified from one to five stars. The rating is always displayed outside as H plus the number of stars. Hotels provide rooms and meals as required in their own restaurant. The larger hotels usually have outdoor swimming pools, tennis courts, shops and entertainment. Many have courtesy buses to take visitors to the beach. Those with three stars or more provide rooms with private bathrooms and toilets. Most have balconies often with sea views. Maid service and laundry should be available.

Hotel apartments

Hotel apartments (*Apartamentos Hoteles* — HA) are similar to hotels but have flats, bungalows or chalets. The star rating is shown after HA.

Resident hotels

These hotels (*Hoteles Residencia* — HR) supply rooms but without restaurant facilities. They usually have less luxurious furnishings though often have private bathrooms and toilets. Shown as HR with star rating.

Guesthouses

Modest hotels and guesthouses (*Hostales* — HS) with star rating of one to three. They provide accommodation with or without meals. They do not have dormitories.

Pensions

Guesthouses (*Pensionés* — P) with a small number of rooms, providing full board.

Residences

These establishments (*Residencias* — R) provide accommodation with a shared bathroom. Breakfast only available.

Inns

Inns (*pousadas, tabernas*) are usually in country districts; the standard is mostly good, but can vary. It is best to view rooms before booking. Often in beautiful surroundings with local atmosphere.

Paradors

A *parador* is the name given to hotels (Parador Nacionales de Turismo) run by the Secretary of State for Tourism in Spain and the Canary Islands. Usually they are in converted historic castles, palaces, convents and monasteries and generally in a location of special scenic beauty or interest. Internal decor is of a luxurious standard, often containing antiques and works of art. They offer every comfort as well as an excellent cuisine. The restaurants are open to non-residents. Sometimes *paradors* can be more expensive than equivalent hotels but they provide a unique tourist experience. It is advisable to book in advance.

The Spanish Tourist Office publishes an informative brochure called *Paradores,* which is given free on request. In the Eastern Canaries there are *paradors* in:

Gran Canaria — Parador Internacional de Tejeda: Two-star Canary style modern building. Bar restaurant, splendid views, high altitude. Tel: 65 80 50 (but at the time of writing the accommodation is closed).

Fuerteventura — Parador Nacional de Fuerteventura: Three-star modern building overlooking Puerto del Rosario and the sea. 24 rooms, swimming pool. Tel: 85 11 50.

Apartments

Self-catering accommodation is available on all the main islands. In the big resorts purpose-built blocks are of enormous size, having their own restaurants, public rooms, swimming pools, sports facilities, supermarket, hairdressing salon and boutique. Some have evening entertainments, such as flamenco shows and music groups.

In the apartments (*Apartamentos*), basic provisions will include bed linen, towels, kitchen equipment and cooking facilities, with cutlery, crockery and glasses. The majority have balconies often with sea views. High rise blocks have lifts. Most provide maid service but in some cases only once a week.

At the reception, details will be found of local entertainment, coach excursions and car hire.

Bungalows and villas

Often built around a swimming pool, bungalows and villas are more attractive as they usually have gardens and shrubs close by. There are always restaurants, bars and supermarkets in the vicinity. Information can be obtained from travel agents *(viajes)*.

Hotels and hotel apartments

Las Palmas

★ ★ ★ ★ ★ **Hotel Melia Las Palmas** Calle Gomera 6, Playa de las Canteras. Tel: 26 76 00. 316 rooms, including suites and conference rooms. Complete room service with mini bar and TV, large pool and sun terrace, cocktail bar and restaurants, garage and Disco El Coto. Facing the Canteras beach and promenade, well established, mainly business hotel. Decor is quiet and formal with courteous service.

★ ★ ★ ★ ★ **Hotel Reina Isabel** Calle Alfredo L Jones 40. Tel: 26 01 00. 260 rooms and suites. Complete room service, TV, facilities for the disabled, convention rooms, shops, roof-top swimming pool, bar and dancing. Pleasant downstairs bar, lounge and terrace facing Canteras beach. Luxurious decor and friendly service.

★ ★ ★ ★ ★ **Hotel Santa Catalina Parque Doramas** Leon y Castillo 227. Tel: 24 30 40. 209 rooms and suites. Casino, restaurant, cocktail bar, convention rooms, swimming pool and tennis courts. Acknowledged the top hotel in Las Palmas and where Royalty stay. The building is historic and beautiful, set in gardens.

★ ★ ★ ★ **Hotel Los Bardinos Sol** Calle Eduardo Benot 5. Tel: 26 61 00. 215 rooms with terrace, TV, video. Conference rooms with audio-visual equipment, swimming pool, boutiques, all well appointed. Circular building, highest hotel in Las Palmas, with disco on 22nd floor. Panorama all over the city and harbour.

★ ★ ★ ★ **Hotel Concorde** Calle Thomas Millar 8. Tel: 26 27 50. 127 rooms. Smart, quiet hotel with solarium, swimming pool, bar, restaurant, music and night club. Close to Canteras beach and port.

★ ★ ★ ★ **Hotel Iberia Sol** Avenida Maritima de Norte. Tel: 36 11 33. 298 rooms, facilities for the disabled, convention halls, restaurant, bars, disco, no garden. Large modern and efficient hotel in Garden City.

★ ★ ★ ★ **Hotel Imperial Playa** Playa de las Canteras 3. Tel: 26 48 54. 173 rooms and suites, with mini bar and safe box. Lounge, Spanish decor, bingo room, hairdresser and massage. Good position in front of Canteras beach.

★ ★ ★ ★ **Hotel Rocamar** Calle Lanzarote 10. Tel: 26 56 00. 77 rooms, bar, restaurant, reading room, night club, no swimming pool but by the Canteras beach.

The view from the Gloria Palace at San Agustin looks over the hotel pool and to the sea, just fifteen minutes walk away.

★ ★ ★ ★ **Hotel Residencia Tigaday** Calle Ripoche 4. Tel: 26 47 20. 160 rooms. Restaurant, bar, night club, entertainments. Overlooking Santa Catalina Park. Convenient for buses, taxis and port but could be noisy.

★ ★ ★ **Hotel Residencia Atlanta** Calle Alfredo L Jones 37. Tel: 26 50 62. 58 rooms. Close to Canteras beach. Small, clean and inexpensive. There are plenty of restaurants and bars nearby.

★ ★ ★ **Hotel Residencia Cantur** Calle Sagastur 28. Tel: 26 34 04. 48 rooms, TV, reading room. By Canteras beach. Simple, inexpensive tourist hotel in convenient position. Bars and restaurants nearby.

★ ★ ★ **Hotel Gran Canaria** Playa de las Canteras 38. Tel: 27 50 78. 90 rooms. Bar, restaurant, air conditioning, TV, reading room, hairdressing, pets allowed. Old established hotel on Canteras seafront.

★ ★ **Hotel Residencia Pujol** Calle Salvador Cuyas 5. Tel: 27 44 33, 48 rooms. TV, restaurant with international and Canarian cuisine. Small, clean with polite and friendly service. Convenient for port and quite close to Canteras beach. Could be noise from traffic.

★ **Hotel Residencia Tamadaba** Calle Pelayo 1. Tel: 26 20 00. 50 rooms. Simple accommodation, telephone in room, money change facility. In central position and open all year. Inland from Canteras beach, off Calle Fernando Guanateme.

San Agustin, Playa del Inglés and Maspalomas

★ ★ ★ ★ ★ **Hotel Maspalomas Oasis** Playa de Maspalomas. Tel: 76 01 70. 274 rooms. The epitome of luxury, this established hotel has a splendid position alongside the sand dunes and is set in exotic tropical gardens. Everything possible for your enjoyment is here, at a price, including sauna, gymnasium, live music and dancing nightly.

★ ★ ★ ★ ★ **Hotel Melia Tamarindos** Calle Retama 3, San Agustin. Tel: 76 26 00. 308 rooms, facilities for the disabled. Swimming pool, tennis and landscaped gardens. At quieter end of the tourist coast, this elegant hotel has all the facilities expected of a five-star establishment. The Casino and La Scala nightclub adjoin.

★ ★ ★ ★ **Hotel Apolo** Avenida de Estados Unidos de America 28, Playa del Inglés. Tel: 76 00 58. 318 rooms and suites. A well appointed busy hotel with plenty of facilities including sauna, gymnasium, tennis, hairdresser and garage. Close to the marvellous beach.

★ ★ ★ ★ **Hotel Costa Canaria** Carretera del Sur Km 61. San Agustin. Tel: 76 02 00. 162 rooms and suites. Three bars, an elegant dining room and lounge. Well established, dignified and quiet hotel, with tropical gardens and tennis courts. The midday buffet is served in the garden. Next door is the night club, La Gruta Pirata.

★ ★ ★ ★ **Hotel Don Gregory** Calle Las Tabaibas 11, San Agustin. Tel: 76 26 68. 245 rooms and suites. Disabled facilities, conference rooms, swimming pool and gardens. A nicely appointed hotel near the Commercial Centre and beach.

★ ★ ★ ★ **Hotel Faro de Maspalomas** Playa Maspalomas. Tel: 76 04 62. 188 rooms overlooking sea and sand dunes. Large swimming pool, shops, hairdresser, gymnasium, night club and garage. This modern hotel caters for all age groups, including the handicapped.

★ ★ ★ ★ **Hotel Gloria Palace** San Agustin. tel: 76 79 29. 448 rooms with balcony and sea view, including junior suites and two presidential suites. Six conference rooms, sport area and disco, all in luxury surroundings. Large and newly opened, the hotel is set back on a hill above San Agustin. Attractive gardens with pools and buffet bar. The service is efficient and friendly.

★ ★ ★ ★ **Hotel Lucana** Plaza del Sol, Playa del Inglés. Tel: 76 27 00. 167 rooms. Garden, swimming pool, tennis, dogs permitted. A modern hotel by the beach.

★ ★ ★ ★ **Hotel Rio Papayas** Avenida Gran Canaria 22, Playa del Inglés. Tel: 76 30 50. Newly opened with adjoining Hotel Apartments Flamingo. The apartments have supermarket, hairdresser and boutiques. They share lush gardens, terraces, swimming pool, solarium and tennis court, dancing nightly and special entertainments, courtesy bus to the beach.

★ ★ ★ **Hotel Beverly Park** Calle Hamburgo, Playa del Inglés. Tel: 76 17 50. 497 rooms. Swimming pool, garden, tennis, mini golf, dancing and entertainments. Very large and well established, family hotel, used by tour operators. Close to beach.

★ ★ ★ **Hotel Continental** Avenida Italia, Playa del Inglés. tel: 76 00 33. 386 rooms. Two swimming pools, sunbed terrace, nightly entertainment. Busy cheerful hotel with relaxed atmosphere, used by package holiday families.

★ ★ ★ **Hotel Eugenia Victoria** Avenida Gran Canaria 26. Playa del Inglés. Tel: 76 25 00. 400 rooms. Public rooms are airconditioned. Swimming pools, tennis, table tennis, petanca, dancing to live band. A comfortable friendly and well established hotel with a free bus to the beach.

★ ★ ★ **Hotel Fiesta Don Miguel** Avenida Tirajana 36, Playa del Inglés. Tel: 76 15 08. 252 rooms and suites. Conference rooms, bars, restaurant, garden, swiming pool, tennis, hairdresser, dogs permitted. Within walking distance of the beach.

★ ★ ★ **Hotel Waikiki** Avenida de Gran Canaria 20, Playa del Inglés.

508 rooms. Large garden with pool and café bar, restaurant, plenty of entertainment. Walking distance to town but further to beach. Singular looking hotel built in circular towers, with tall totem pole outside.

★ ★ ★ **Hotel Apartments Buenaventura** Plaza de Ansite, Playa del Inglés. Tel: 76 16 50. 1432 rooms. Large pool and facilities for the disabled. Long established and used by package tour operators. This is a pleasant family hotel with entertainments and amusements. Courtesy bus goes to the beach.

Elsewhere in the island

● Agaete

★ ★ **Hotel Princes Guayarmina** Los Berrazales. Tel: 89 80 09. 27 rooms including two singles. A modest hotel with bar, restaurant and TV. A delightfully peaceful situation in tropical valley. Once a spa hotel.

● Barranco Los Palmitos

Hotel Helga Mastoff Tennis Club Palmitos Park. Tel: 76 14 36. Correspondence to Apartado 176, Maspalomas. 20 rooms with balcony. Restaurant bar, swimming pool, sauna and tennis school. Set in a marvellous position, high up in the *barranco*.

● Mogán and Puerto Rico

★ ★ ★ **Hotel Apartments Club de Mar** Playa de Mogán. Tel: 74 01 00. This smart new hotel has a swimming pool in attractive garden, sauna and gymnasium, evening entertainment. Hotel shops include a hairdresser. Situated right by the modern yacht marina and port, close to small beach.

★ ★ **Hotel Apartments Puerto Plata** Avenida de la Cornisa, Puerto Rico. Tel: 74 51 50. 68 rooms. Swimming pool and sun terrace, hairdressing salon. In an elevated position on the western slopes, with fine views over the harbour and Puerto Rico.

★ **Hotel Apartments La Riviera** Playa del Cura (near Tauro). Tel: 74 51 31. 70 rooms. Swimming pool in garden surroundings. This long established modest hotel, popular with a regular German clientele, is right on the beach, close to the main road between Puerto Rico and Mogan.

● Santa Brigida

★ ★ ★ **Hotel Banadama Golf** Bandama, Santa Brigida. Tel: 35 33 54. 40 rooms including one suite. Heated swimming pool, solarium, sauna, tennis courts, telex and fax service. Meals are served in the Clubhouse restaurant. A quiet modern hotel in the grounds of Spain's oldest golf course. High up on the edge of an extinct volcano. A wonderful location, yet just fifteen minutes drive from Las Palmas.

● Tafira Alta

★**Hotel Apartments Los Frailes** Carretera del Centro Km8. Tel: 35 12 06. 26 rooms.

Apartments

Las Palmas

★ ★ ★**Aguas Verdes** Canteras 47. Tel: 26 84 50. 104 apartments, studio, one bed and two bed, not all with sea view, lift.

★ ★ ★**Farylaga Playa** Calle Alfredo L Jones. Tel: 27 18 00. 29 one, two and three bed luxury apartments, close to the Canteras beach. Lift, restaurant and hairdresser.

★ ★ **Turismar** Calle Sargento Llagas 33. Tel: 27 58 08. Studio and two bed apartments, situated in busy street, five minutes from the Canteras beach.

Playa de las Canteras, a bay of golden sand, is one of Gran Canaria's most famous beaches. It has a long promenade and safe swimming.

The number of apartments available in the south is enormous, with some projects having six thousand beds. Travel agents and tourist information offices will have lists and addresses, or a friendly taxi driver may help in your selection. All developments have swimming pool and sunbathing terraces, most have bars and restaurants, usually there is a supermarket nearby.

Playa del Inglés
★ ★ ★ **Paraiso Maspalomas** Avenida Gran Canaria. Tel: 76 23 00. 423 apartments with TV and telephone. Well situated near the centre of town, with nearby shops, restaurants, cafés and bars. Very pleasant gardens.

Pensions
Pensions (guesthouses) do not officially exist in the south of the island. For Las Palmas the Tourist Office recommend the following which are all in the city near San Telmo Park.
— Calle Eusebio Navarro 11. Tel: 36 04 52
— Calle Perojo 19. Tel: 37 29 60
— Calle Mayor de Triana 79. Tel: 36 04 72

Camping

Camping rules that apply in mainland Spain also apply in the Canary Islands. A copy of the camping regulations should be carried by anyone intending to camp in the Canaries. This can be obtained from:
The Spanish Tourist Office 57-58 St James's Street, London SW1A 1LD. Tel: 071-499 0901.

The official list of campsites in Spain shows three sites in the Canary Islands: Camping Nauta, Canada Blanca, in Tenerife; and Camping Guantanamo, Tauro, and Camping Temisas, Temisas, in Gran Canaria. In fact, a fourth official camping park has been opened at Pasito Blanco in the south of Gran Canaria. However, the site at Temisas was found to be closed in the early spring of 1990, with no indication as to when it will be re-opened, despite the Tourist Office statement that it is officially open, with a reasonable service. Incidentally this site in the mountains has a difficult approach for caravans and larger motorhomes. Because of the lack of campsites, off site camping is tolerated in all the Canary Islands, provided campers behave in an appropriate manner.

It is not necessary to have a Camping Carnet, but it is an advantage, particularly for those who camp outside sites, as third party insurance is included. Camping Carnets can be obtained from camping and motoring organisations such as the AA, RAC and Caravan Club, and cost approximately £2. A passport-size photo is required.

Camping on site

You will be required to present your passport at the camp site reception. Persons under the age of 16 may not be admitted unless accompanied by an adult. Silence must be respected between 2300 and 0800 hours. Fires are not permitted except in allocated places. Campers are not allowed to carry offensive weapons. Valuables may be left with the camp manager for safe keeping. Most sites have their own post boxes and supermarkets. Every reception office has an official complaints book.

Camping off site

Camping is allowed outside official camp sites provided one has the permission of the owner of the land. Areas where most campers tend to congregate are in the south of Tenerife and the south of Gran Canaria but, generally speaking, campers are accepted on all the islands (although Canarians would prefer the visitors used the hotels, villas and apartments). We advise campers to seek the advice of the local police when they wish to camp in this way.

No more than three units may camp together for more than three days outside a site and the number must not exceed ten persons.

Camping is not allowed in the following places: on dry river beds and seasonal flooding areas; within military, industrial or tourist areas; within a radius of 150 metres from the source of a town's water supply; within urban areas or unreasonably near the roadside; within one kilometre of an official camp site.

Hints for campers

One of the main requirements of all campers is water, which, in the Canary Islands, is in short supply. Therefore it is necessary to conserve and plan ahead. Most petrol filling stations will allow containers to be filled but make sure that it is drinking water (*agua potable*) or buy bottled water from a supermarket. Camping 'Gaz' is available in towns and some villages. A 907 refill costs 350 pesetas.

Further information on camping in the Canary Islands can be obtained from periodicals such as *Caravan; Camping and Walking;*

Motorcaravan and Motorhome Monthly; Which Motorcaravan, Motorcaravan and *Motorcaravan World.*

Backpackers

Since camping is not permitted in most tourist areas campers are not welcome on many beaches. In the past, the 'hippy' type of backpacker has caused the authorities much trouble: hence the reluctance to let groups of campers forgather. However, backpackers do visit the islands, using simple hostels with the odd night camping; but care is required in conforming with the regulations.

Caravans

The terrain of the Canary Islands is not conducive to touring with a towed caravan, so these are mostly taken to Camping Guantanamo, Tauro, or Camping Pasito Blanco (or Camping Nauta in Tenerife), or after using the caravan to cross Europe, their owners stay at a rented apartment or villa. A few hardy caravanners may find quiet places which are suitable for a short stay, having obtained permission from the police or the owner: these sites, usually on waste ground, are few and far between.

At present there are no official camping places in Lanzarote or Fuerteventura. The authorities are aware of this and tolerate free parking on some beaches when it is not causing a public nuisance. Motorcaravan windsurf enthusiasts tend to visit Lanzarote and Fuerteventura where there are windsurfing schools. They favour La Santa, Costa Teguise and Puerto del Carmen on Lanzarote. In Fuerteventura, Corralejo, Playa del Castillo and Jandia Playa are popular places. We have always enjoyed our motorcaravan holidays on all the Canary Islands.

Certainly the most suitable way to camp in the Canary Islands is to use a motorcaravan. The diversity of scenery and regions makes travelling interesting and varied. Provided one parks with consideration to the regulations there should be few problems.

The camp sites in Gran Canaria

• **Camping Pasito Blanco** is a Class 1 site situated opposite the yacht club marina in the south, between Maspalomas and Arguineguin. Set on dry hillside, most of the pitches are terraced and well lit. The whole camp has a perimeter fence. There are many static units and some have small gardens. Facilities on camp include a reception, modern toilet block with hot showers, a large restaurant open from 1200 to 2300 hrs, supermarket, laundry and a large

swimming pool. A bus stop is close to the camp entrance. Charges
per day:

Persons, 325 pesetas (£1.67) adult, 150 pesetas (£0.77) child.

Motorcaravan, 600 pesetas (£3.09) to 800 pesetas (£4.12)

Caravan and car, 800 pesetas (£4.12)

Electricity, 160 pesetas (£0.82)

Reductions are made for stays over one month.

● **Camping Guantanamo,** Tauro Class 3a, is owned by a Canarian
who lives in Las Palmas. In fact the camp consists of three separate
sites. The original **Guantanamo Camp One** is situated on the seaside
of the main Puerto Rico to Mogán road and is used mainly by
'backpackers' and 'tenters'. It has some permanent caravans owned
by Canarians; there are also a few 'cells' for rent — these are just
bare rooms that can be locked; no beds are provided and they can
be booked in advance.

On the camp the facilities are sparse. Basins and showers have
cold water only (but with the climate being so pleasant this is not
a great hardship). Sinks are provided for dish and clothes washing.
Open wood fires give communal cooking facilities. Toilets are
adequate, except when the camp is overcrowded, usually at
Christmas time. Recently a supermarket and bar restaurant have
been built adjoining the main road.

The restaurant is under separate management and service is of a
high standard with a friendly atmosphere, delicious food and an
interesting menu. Price of a main course is about 600 pesetas/£3.09.
It is open to non-campers.

Tents are pitched on very hard ground. Some are sited in the
shade under trees or straw awnings, other places are without shade.
Predominantly, a younger type of camper uses Camp One. Parties
and 'sing-songs' are organised amongst themselves. The beach,
which runs around a horse-shoe bay, is a mixture of sand and
pebble and suitable for swimming. At one end are two bars, and
adjoining the camp, on the beach, is a small shop with a verandah
where campers may enjoy a drink, or sit and watch the sunset.

Camp Two is across the main road, opposite Camp One, behind
high concrete walls with gates that are closed at night. Tents are not
allowed, though awnings attached to caravans and motorcaravans
are permitted. Marked pitches are sheltered by tall trees and the
camp is swept clean every day.

A modern toilet block has cold showers, basins for washing,
laundry and chemical toilet disposal. Electric points are available
(220 volts) and the power is on from 1800 to 2300 hrs. This camp
becomes very full over the Christmas period.

Motorcaravaners from northern Europe and elsewhere, seen here about to board the ferry at Cadiz, are frequent visitors to Gran Canaria, especially in winter time.

Camp Three is located about three kilometres inland, along the valley *(barranco)* in an unusual and attractive setting, with dry volcanic mountains on three sides — a sheltered situation. This site, opened in autumn 1982, is very level and clean and, provided one does not mind a venue a few miles from the sea, it makes a pleasant and peaceful place to camp. Here both tents and vans are allowed.

The newly built toilet block has flush toilets and wash basins with cold water taps. Some showers have hot water for which an extra charge is made. Electricity is available from 1800 to 2300 hrs. A delivery daily of fresh bread and eggs is made and a travelling greengrocery van arrives twice a week.

Although part of the site is level and shaded with many trees, at times it can be dusty. The rest of the camp is terraced with views of the mountains. A decent sized swimming pool is also a good place to sunbathe. Interesting walks can be had in the volcanic terrain; be sure to wear stout footwear and if the weather is hot take a sunhat. This third camp, now called Annexo II, can become busy at weekends with local Canarian campers.

Most of the camp is full with static or long stay Canarian campers. only a small nucleus of British campers are regulars. It should be pointed out that this camp is of a lower standard than most in Europe, but the setting in the valley is pleasant and the climate is the big attraction. The approach road of about two kilometres is rough, narrow and winding, though not impossible for towed caravans and large motorhomes. Charges per day: Two persons, car and caravan, 780 pesetas (£4.02); Two persons and motorcaravan, 780 pesetas (£4.02); Electricity (on from 1400 to 1600 and 1830 to 2330 hrs), 160 pesetas (£0.82); Hot shower, 100 pesetas (£0.50).

Travel agents' services

There are numerous travel agents (*viajes*) in the tourist parts of the Canary Islands. Their services are varied; they are agents for hotels, apartments, ferry and flight bookings, car hire, coach tours and currency exchange. Open from 0900 to 1300 and 1630 to 1900 hrs, Monday to Friday. 0900 to 1300 hrs on Saturday and closed on Sundays and Public Holidays.

British-run Viajes Blandy, Fernando Poo and Wagonlit Cooks have branches in Gran Canaria and Tenerife. Other well established firms are Viajes Cyrasa, Melia, Insular and Ultramar Express. The latter two firms have English-speaking staff and run many excursions throughout the islands with coaches that are modern and comfortable. Some addresses are:

Barcelo Parrque Santa Catalina, Las Palmas. Tel: 27 74 92.

El Corte Inglés Avenida Mesa y Lopez, 18. Las Palmas. Tel: 27 60 00.

Insular Calle Luis Morote 9, Las Palmas. Tel: 23 31 44. Also at Carretera General, Maspalomas. Tel: 76 05 00, and Centro Commercial, Puerto Rico. Tel: 74 50 18.

Ultramar Express Calle Luis Morote 37, Las Palmas. Tel: 23 31 44, 27 27 10. Also at Edificio Mercurio, Avenida Tirajana, Playa del Inglés.

Package holidays

There are many UK firms operating package holidays to the Canary Islands. These provide a wide choice of selection and offer good value to holidaymakers with a limited amount of time. They also enable customers to budget in advance for most of their holiday expenses.

When you book a package holiday, the price of the air fare is included, plus transport to and from your destination, unless otherwise stated. Tour operators' brochures will give details of flight arrangements, type of resort, entertainments and the star rating of the accommodation. These vary from five-star luxury hotels to modest guesthouses, self-catering apartments and villas. In some instances it is possible to visit more than one island during your holiday.

At present the islands of Tenerife and Gran Canaria have the most package tours available, with Lanzarote a very popular third choice. Fuerteventura has recently entered the tourist market and now has hotels in both the north and south. Gomera and El Hierro are not at present included in package holiday programmes, but no doubt it will happen in due course.

In the larger resorts and holiday complexes like Puerto de la Cruz, Tenerife and Playa del Inglés, Gran Canaria, entire hotels and apartment blocks are taken over by the tour operator and prove so popular that they are full for most of the year. The cheaper high season packages are for simple self-catering apartments and cost about £225 per person sharing a double room or apartment for two weeks. Hotels will cost about £275 to £350 for the same period but can increase to £500. (One has to remember that the Canary Islands are a 4½-hour flight from London, which makes it a more expensive journey than one to the Mediterranean.)

Amongst the tour operators offering Canary Island packages are: Airways, Cosmos, Enterprise, Ingram, Lanzarote Villas, Lanzotic Travel, Mundi Color, Portland, Scotia, Silvair, Sovereign, Student Travel, Thomas Cook, Travel Club, Tjaereborg, Thomson Holidays, Wings, Yorkshire Travel. Check with you local travel agents for up-to-date details of package holidays.

Saga Holidays offer package deals for the 'over 60s', to Tenerife and Gran Canaria during 'off-peak' periods.

Property and real estate agents

The Canary Islands present an appealing location for purchasers to invest in property, but it is advisable to get specialist advice on the subject.

Selling apartments, bungalows and villas, the administration of properties, letting, legal advice, repairs, technical services and insurance, are all transactions, carried out by real estate companies in the Canary Islands, and most of the firms employ multi-lingual staff, trained to assist clients.

'Time sharing' is on the increase and firms like Wimpey have recently entered the market. *Urbanizaciónes,* as property developments are called, tend to group in nationalities in particular areas.

The British appear to favour Puerto de la Cruz and Playa de las Americas in Tenerife. Gran Canaria has British residents in the Tafira district of Las Palmas, in Playa del Inglés and Puerto Rico. A big proportion of British residents like Lanzarote where English is well understood.

Real estate companies and agents where English is spoken are:
● Gran Canaria
Imobiliaria Roca Avenida Maritima del Norte, Las Palmas Tel: 21 65 00
Agencia Zabolota Reloj 2, Las Palmas Tel: 31 49 22.
Immobiliaria PJ Barber Edificio Prisma, Playa del Inglés. Tel: 76 54 47
● Lanzarote
Lanzarote Villas, 37 East Street, Horsham, Sussex, UK. Tel: 51304.
● Tenerife
Tim Wise,, Immobiliaria Concay, Edificio Iguazu, Calle Enrique Talg, (PO Box) Apartado 670, Puerto de la Cruz. Tel: 37 14 52 and 37 21 06.

Time share

Time share is the ownership of a property (apartment or bungalow) for any period you care to purchase, such as a week, a month or more in a year. There is a once only purchase payment, and then an annual fee to cover management, maintenance, electricity and water. It is a modern way to own a holiday home for the purchased period and you are free to use it as you wish. Such properties are to be found in Gran Canaria in places like Maspalomas, Puerto Rico and Puerto Mogán. The purchase cost for a one-bedroom apartment for one week annually could be about £4,000. You are strongly advised to seek qualified advice before signing any documents.

FOUR

Getting about in the Canaries

There are no trains in the Canary Islands so you have to get about by road. Fortunately the main roads and motorways are good, and *autopistas* (motorways) are free of tolls. Traffic is only heavy in cities and towns but the driving is well disciplined. However roads in the country are sometimes little more than rough tracks across desert land and progress can be slow.

A good map of the Canary Islands is therefore essential. Recommended is the series published by Firestone Hispania available in the Canary Islands from petrol filling stations and bookshops. In Great Britain and Ireland they can be obtained from bookshops with a strong foreign map section or direct, by post, from the agent, Roger Lascelles (Dept Firestone) 47 York Road, Brentford, Middlesex, TW8 0QP. Tel: 081-847 0935. Map references are: T-32 Canary Islands; E-50 Tenerife;and E-51 Gran Canaria.

Another useful map is in the Daily Telegraph, Spanish Leisure Map Series, entitled *Gran Canaria,* also obtainable from Roger Lascelles.

Driving in Spain and the Canary Islands

If you are taking a car to the Canary Islands, driving through Spain and taking the car ferry from Cadiz to either Tenerife or Gran Canaria, you will require the following:
1   Driving Licence
2   International Driving Permit
3   Green Card Insurance (your insurance company issues this)
4   Bail Bond (from AA, RAC or insurance company — this is an indemnity if you are involved in an accident)
5   Vehicle Registration Document

6   Passport
7   A spare set of light bulbs (Spanish law requirement)
8   A red triangle, for warning of breakdown obstruction
9   Means of changing direction of headlight dip
10 GB sticker

Police patrol on motorcycles, especially on the Carretera General (main road) and the Autopista (motorway). The maximum speed in towns and villages is 40kph, elsewhere 100kph. Traffic offences are fined on the spot by Traffic Police. Amongst the traffic offences you can be fined for are not wearing seat belts, and parking on white and yellow lines. Fines can cost up to 10,000 pesetas (£50). There is a 10 per cent reduction if you pay immediately, so it is advisable to carry some pesetas as well as your passport and driving licence.

Up to date information on this subject is best obtained from the AA, RAC or the Spanish Tourist Office. However, the following points are worthy of note:

● Drive on the right-hand side of the road.
● Sound your horn when overtaking.
● Stop for pedestrians on crossings.
● Wear seatbelts.
● Only sidelights required in built up areas.
● Do not cross the single white line, it is equivalent to the double white line in the UK.
● Observe the no overtaking signs, and speed limits.
● Give way to traffic coming from the right, particularly at roundabouts.

Road signs

Most road signs are international. One important traffic control is the *cambio de sentido* (change direction), generally controlled by traffic lights, which prevents vehicles turning across oncoming traffic or from doing a U-turn. Here are some road sign translations:

Aduana   customs post
Aparcamiento   parking
Atencíon   caution
Blandones   soft verges
Cedo el Paso   give way
Derecha   right
Despacio   slow
Desvio   diversion
Escuela   school

Estacionamiento prohibido   no parking
Izquierda left
Obras workmen
Pare stop
Paso prohibido   No thoroughfare
Peatones   pedestrians
Peligro danger
Peligroso dangerous
Salidas exit

Petrol filling stations

In the Canary Islands most petrol filling stations are closed all day
on Sundays and public holidays. Those that stay open are advertised
in the local Spanish press, such as *La Provincia*. In addition there
are several that are open twenty-four hours and these are becoming
more frequent. They do not provide car repair services; this is a
separate service, *taller mechanico*. Good toilets and drinking water
can be found at filling stations. Autoshops sell spares and sweets.
Car wash services are similar to those in the UK.

Petrol comes in three grades, Extra 98 Octane, Super 96 Octane,
and Normal 92 Octane. At present the price of Super is 58 pesetas
(30) a litre. Do not confuse petrol (*gasolina*) with diesel (*gasoil*).
Lead free is expected to be introduced during 1990.

Car servicing and repairs

There are plenty of places for servicing and repairing cars. The cities
of Tenerife and Gran Canaria have agents for most well-known
British and foreign cars. There could be some delay in obtaining a
particular spare part required from abroad.

In country places a small workshop (*taller mechanico*), which
deals with local vehicles, will assist. The standard is good and
repairs are promptly effected. Costs are usually more reasonable
than in the UK. Facilities for tyre fitting, battery charging and car
washing are available.

Car hire (self drive)

Car hire firms in the Canary Islands include international names like
Hertz and Avis, Organización Canaria Coches Aquiler (abbrev-
iation OCCA) and local firms. Prices vary, so it is worth shopping
around if you are in a large resort like Playa del Inglés in Gran
Canaria. The type of cars range from a luxury Mercedes to a safari
jeep. Costs will vary with the make and size of vehicle — for
example:

— Seat Marbella, per day, 2,700 pesetas (£13.91); per week, 13,300 pesetas (£68.85).
— Opel Corsa or open Marbella, per day, 3,200 pesetas (£16.49); per week, 20,300 pesetas (£104.63).
— Ford Fiesta 1.0 or Renault S5, per day, 3,500 pesetas (£18); per week, 22,400 pesetas (£115.46).
— Ford Escort or Ibiza 1.5, per day, 4,100 pesetas (£21.13); per week, 26,600 pesetas (£137).
— Opel Kadett 1.6, per day, 4,500 pesetas (£23.19); per week, 28,700 pesetas (£147.93).
— Jeep Suzuki or Mini Moke, per day, 5,000 pesetas (£15.77); per week, 32,200 pesetas (£166).
— Mini Bus 9 seats, per day, 7,000 pesetas (£36); per week, 46,900 pesetas (£242).

To these costs a tax (ITE) of 4 per cent is added. Payment can usually be made by credit card or Eurocheque. Motorcycles, scooters and bicycles can also be rented. (Crash helmets have to be worn on motorcycles.)

Note that it is not advisable to drive your car off the road and on to the beaches or rough tracks as the insurance may not cover you for this purpose. If you have a Jeep make sure that the insurance covers you for safari type drives. Also, understand your contract, it should be written in English. A deposit of 5,000 pesetas (£26) is sometimes required. Vehicle insurance usually costs about 500 pesetas (£2.57) a day depending on the class of vehicle. Personal insurance costs about 250 pesetas (£1.28) per day and covers all occupants. Generally you are required to be over twenty-one years of age and to have held a driving licence for one year. It is not necessary to have an International Driving Permit, though your own licence will need to be produced, likewise your passport. Most firms will deliver and collect vehicles. This includes the airport. It may be cheaper and simpler to arrange your car hire with your travel agent in the UK and collect it at the airport. Avis are one of the firms that can arrange this for you.

If you are unfortunate to have an accident do not leave your vehicle, and if anyone is injured do not attempt to move them, but call an ambulance and inform the police.

Car hire firms in Gran Canaria include:

Avis Airport, Tel: 70 01 57; Las Palmas, Tel: 26 55 72; Playa del Inglés, Tel: 76 14 54; San Agustin, Tel: 76 27 93.
Hertz San Agustin, Tel: 70 00 84; Playa del Inglés, Tel: 76 24 03.
OCCA Puerto Rico, Tel: 74 57 16.

Cicar Playa del Inglés, Tel: 76 15 34.
Inter Canarias Airport, Tel: 70 01 73; Puerto Rico, Tel: 74 57 21.

Buses

Gran Canaria and Tenerife are well provided with public bus services; in the other islands the service is adequate. Bus stops are marked, sometimes by *Parada* (stopping place). You always enter a bus from the front and buy your ticket from the conductor or driver; only single journey (*ida*) tickets are issued. Remember to retain your ticket as inspectors cover all routes. Canary bus queues are usually orderly and line up facing the direction in which the bus will travel. For long distances there are fast buses having limited stops, sometimes marked *Expres* or *Directo*. Buses run every day including Public Holidays. Timetables can be obtained from Tourist Offices and some bus terminals. Fares are not expensive.

Vehicles range from comfortable long distance coaches to ancient bone-shakers. The Canarians call their buses *guaguas* (pronounced 'wah wah') but *autobus* is generally understood.

In Gran Canaria bus routes are centred on Las Palmas. City buses run from Parque Santa Catalina. The airport service starts from the Iberia Office, Calle Leon y Castillo, and country routes run from the bus terminal at Calle Rafael Cabrera, near the Parque de San Telmo.

The bus services to the south include direct fast routes between Las Palmas, Playa del Inglés and Maspalomas, every fifteen minutes from 0615 and 2200 hrs. The service between Las Palmas and Puerto Rico is half hourly from 0530 to 2200 hrs. Between Las Palmas and Telde every fifteen minutes. In Telde, Vecindario and Maspalomas there are connecting buses up into the mountains from the south.

Routes from Las Palmas covering the north include Tejeda, Agaete and San Nicolás de Tolentino, passing through Arucas, Guía and Gálder. From Gálder there are auxiliary routes to towns in the north. Practically every village and town on the island can be reached by bus, given time.

Do not rely on bus timetables being accurate, one needs to enquire, especially at weekends and on public holidays. Do not leave it until the last scheduled bus before returning to your resort. For information on bus timetables in Las Palmas telephone 36 86 31; in Telde 69 19 87; in Vecindario 75 04 66; and in Playa del Inglés 76 53 59 or 76 53 32.

Taxis

Taxis are a pleasure to use on the Canary Islands and give a good but not always cheap service. Generally they are large Mercedes and kept very clean by their Canarian drivers. You may have to listen to taped Canarian music and some drivers do not allow smoking. At night most display a green light as being available for hire, also there is a sign indicating 'free' (*libre*). Taxis in the larger towns have meters and the drivers are very good at giving change, though they expect a tip (*propina*) of about ten per cent.

For those taxis that do not have meters, or if you wish to go beyond the city or town limits, it is necessary to arrange the price beforehand. Misunderstandings usually occur because of lack of communication; some drivers will write down the price and place, which is helpful. Baggage may require a surcharge of about 40 pesetas (20p) per item. Typical fares (at time of writing):

— Airport to Las Palmas, 2,500 pesetas (£12.88); to Playa del Inglés, 3,000 pesetas (£15.46).

— Playa del Inglés to San Agustin, 400 pesetas (£2.06); to Maspalomas, 450 pesetas (£2.31); to Las Palmas, 4,000 pesetas (£20.61).

To call a Radio Taxi telephone 27 77 12, 27 77 53 or 27 78 07.

Tartanas

In Las Palmas de Gran Canaria, horse drawn carriages (*tartanas*) used to be found on the Calle Simon Bolivar, opposite Plaza Santa Catalina. These gaily decorated open carriages allowed you to view at a slow pace the seafront, docks, market and city centre. At present there is only one there, maybe the volume of traffic has proved too much for their excursions. A *tartana* can carry four persons and the price should be previously arranged. A tip is expected.

Excursions

There is no doubt that one of the easiest ways of enjoying the sights of Gran Canaria, and the Canary Islands, is to take a coach tour or sea cruise. These facilities are offered as half day, whole day and evening excursions and are well advertised in hotels, apartments, travel agents and local papers. When on a package holiday your tour representative is sure to describe what can be seen and will be glad to make your reservation. Should you be an independent traveller you can still join these tours, assuming there is a vacant seat.

Make sure that you book an excursion that has an English-speaking guide and check whether the cost includes a meal. Remember to take your sunglasses, camera, cardigan or pullover. Possibly flat shoes and a towel if the excursrion includes visiting a beach or a boat trip. Most days it is sensible to take a sun hat, since even when it is not bright the sun's rays can filter through the clouds.

Your tour is likely to stop at an *artesania* (souvenir shop) so some extra cash may be required (though most accept credit cards) for this, also for snacks and cold drinks en route. If you have young children some bottled water and sweets will be appreciated. As well as coach and sea excursions, air tours can be enjoyed from Gran Canaria to Lanzarote, Fuerteventura and Tenerife, either for a day, or possibly involving a night stop.

Here are some examples of excursions available. Prices may vary according to starting points: these listed are from Playa del Inglés, where Ultramar Express and Insular travel agents organise excursions with English-speaking guides.

Anchors Away A full day trip at sea, aboard an old schooner, sailing along the coast, including lunch with wine and entertainments. Fun for all the family. 3,500 pesetas (£18).

Gran Canary Discovery Round the island coach tour with stops to visit banana plantations, tourist shops, churches and viewpoints, lunch included. 3,500 pesetas (£18).

Palmitos Park A visit to the Parrot Park is a leisurely excursion. Free buses run with several pick up points in Playa del Inglés. A taxi from San Agustin would cost 1,220 pesetas (£6.28). To drive to the Parrot Park, take the main road out of Playa del Inglés, south. The route is well sign-posted on the right and up the barranco. Entrance costs 850 pesetas (£4.38). The botanical gardens and park have 1,400 exotic birds. Some are caged but over 400 fly freely, the flamingoes being especially beautiful. Every day there are several shows when ten parrots entertain with marvellous tricks. There is also an excellent collection of cacti and agaves.

Ocean Park A large water park south of Playa del Inglés, with water splash, big dipper and all the usual attractions, sun beds, cafeteria and restaurant. Open from 1,000 to 1,900 hrs, entrance costs 1,300 pesetas (£6.70), children 695 pesetas (£3.58).

Jeep Safari Ten jeeps tour for seventy five kilometres on out of the way roads and tracks, stopping for lunch and tea. 3,500 pesetas (£18).

Reptilandia Park An unusual zoo with reptiles in natural surroundings and an indoor visitors' centre of poisonous snakes and frogs. One hundred different species. Splendid views. Entrance costs 400 pesetas (£2.06), children half price. Signposted on the right from Galder, on the main road to Agaete. Open from 1100 to 1730 hrs.

Sand Dune Camel Safari Half day excursion sitting on top of a camel, plodding amongst the sand dunes of Maspalomas, followed by a barbecue with sangría. 2,600 pesetas (£13.40).

Sioux City In the Canon del Aguila, well signposted on the main San Agustin to Playa del Inglés road Km48, an old film set is now used for a Wild West show. Visitors can see great feats of horsemanship, knife throwing, lassoing from horseback, a 'bank robbery', cattle-herding and many other exciting daredevil deeds. Tourists can walk up the main street of this cowboy village and visit Western-style bars and shops, church and corals. In the 'hotel' meals and drinks are served. Open from 1000 hrs, shows at 1200 and 1530 hrs. Several nights a week 'barbecue parties' are held:

Schoolchildren admire the clifftop scenery before being taken round the Reptilandia park, where hundreds of small reptiles are kept in natural surroundings.

entrance cost includes whisky, chicken, pork chops, steaks, potatoes, salad, plus a banana! Later there is a sparkling show by Tom Leddas and family, Mexicans of great daring and skill. Free drinks and dancing continue until midnight. Entrance costs 4,200 pesetas (£21.64), including meal.

Tropical Gardens Trip Half-day visit to the Botanical Gardens, Jardin Canario, near Santa Brigida, where many tropical Canarian plants grow in natural settings. Small visitors centre and restaurant. 2,600 pesetas (£13.40). Should you wish to drive there it has two entrances, one on the Las Palmas to Santa Brigida road at Km7, the other on the Almatriche to La Cazada road at Km7. Admission is free, open from 0800 to 1730 hrs on week days, Saturdays 0800 to 1200 and 1500 to 1900 hrs.

Volcanic Experience This coach excursion takes you into the centre of Gran Canaria, to see the volcanic craters and high mountains. A typical Canarian luncheon is included. Take a sweater as it can be cool in high places. 3,400 pesetas (£17.52).

Twentieth Century Stonehenge This rather fanciful name means you will tour the south of the island, see Guanche caves and visit a Guanche museum in the pretty village of Santa Lucia. Lunch is served at an outdoor patio in a rustic restaurant. 2800 pesetas (£14.43).

Other excursions are available, such as the popular donkey safaris at Aguimes and El Tablero, and the various sea trips from Puerto Rico. All these are well advertised. Day excursions to other islands can be made by jetfoils and aeroplane (see Chapter 2); these inter island flights are very quick and allow plenty of time for sight seeing and shopping. Even more venturesome are the air trips to Fez in Morocco, with a drive through the desert; or to The Gambia for lunch and dinner, if you have loads of pesetas!

Lateen sailing

Canarian lateen sailing is a sport unique to Gran Canaria. With a boat of short length and an area of sail exaggerated for the breadth of the boat, islanders challenge nature when the trade winds blow from April to September. They demonstrate a great deal of skill and risk. The regattas take place in the Bay of Las Palmas and can be seen from all along the Avenida Maritima.

FIVE

Food, drink and entertainment

Buying food

The Canary Islands, because of their free ports, have a great variety of food and drink. The tourist areas, especially, are full of exotic foodstuffs from all over the world. Las Palmas, with its international traffic, offers an enormous selection of gourmet and epicure foods.

Prices of imported foods from Spain tend to be higher than on the mainland. Most other food prices are comparable with, if not cheaper than, Europe. Of course, if you buy a tin of baked beans with an English brand name, then it will be more expensive than a similar product bearing a Canarian or Spanish brand name.

Meat (*carne*) is plentiful. Local Canarian pork (*cerdo*) is excellent: pork chops (*chuleta de cerda*) are on every menu. Beef (*carne de vacca*) is of good quality and imported from Brazil. There is no problem with getting it minced (*carne picada*). Lamb (*cordero*) and mutton (*carne de carnero*) are rather more expensive. Liver (*hígado*) and kidneys (*rinón*) are cheap and tasty. Chickens (*pollo*) are plentiful, fresh or frozen. Very succulent is young goat or kid (*cabrito*) which is roasted on special festive occasions. Rabbit (*conejo*) is much used for stews.

Fish (*pescado*) is found in all towns and villages, though sometimes supplies run out early in the day. Prices are high owing to the demand. Varieties include, tuna (*atun*), cod (*bacalad*), hake (*merluza*), swordfish (*espada*), mackerel (*caballa*) and sardines (*sardinas*). It is possible to go to the fishing villages and buy fish straight off the boats but the prices remain high.

Cheese (*queso*) is imported from many countries and Dutch cheese can be bought more cheaply here than in Holland. Goat's cheese (*queso blanco de cabra*), mainly from the smaller islands of El Hierro and La Palma, is particulary flavoursome.

Milk (*leche*) is not often sold fresh, as there are few cows on the islands. Most milk is 'long-life' imported from Holland in cartons or plastic containers. Tinned and powdered milk are also available.

Bread (*pan*) is sold in most supermarkets, but the place to buy really fresh bread, including brown, is a baker's shop (*panadería*). Rolls and bread are light but not crusty as French bread. Cakes may be bought from a *pasteleria*. These do not usually sell bread as well, but have a selection of sweets and chocolates (*confites y bombón*).

Various brands of tea and coffee are on sale, including ground coffee and Nescafé, the latter a little dearer than in the UK. Excellent local and Spanish honey (*meil*) can be bought; the date palm honey (*meil de palma*) has an unusual flavour.

There is plenty of fresh fruit and vegetables. This is best bought in the open markets but supermarkets in the tourist centres are well supplied. The selection is wide, so enjoy fresh strawberries and pineapples at Christmas time!

Local dishes

It is possible to have typical British meals in Gran Canaria. 'Real English Breakfast' signs are displayed in all tourist resorts. Most hotel restaurants serve food that tends to be bland; trying to please all their customers, they refrain from too much flavour.

Local dishes often include *papas arrugadas* (wrinkled potatoes) — quite delicious little new potatoes cooked in their skins in sea- or salt-water; these should be eaten with their skins on. Served with chops or fish, they will be accompanied by a Canarian piquant sauce called *mojo,* made of oil, vinegar, salt, pimento and spices. *Mojo picon* is red and hot, *mojo verde* is green and milder; often the sauces vary according to the cook. The sauce can be obtained in supermarkets, a small bottle costing about 150 pesetas (76p).

Familiar Spanish dishes include *gazpacho* — a tasty cold soup made from tomatoes, onions, pimentos, olive oil and sherry; and *paella* — rice cooked with saffron to which are added meats, fish and vegetables. *Tortilla* can be a simple omelette becoming *tortilla espanola* when potatoes, onions and vegetables are added.

Canarian soups (*sopa*) are tasty and almost a complete meal, so many good things are included. The one that is recommended to tourists is *sopa de berros,* watercress soup with herbs.

Stews (*puchero* or *estofado*) are considered a main dish; often made with rabbit (*estofado de conjero*), they are eaten with *gofio,* a meal made from wheat or maize which is toasted before being ground, and then made into a sort of dumpling, or sometimes eaten as bread.

Fish stew (*cazuela canaria*) is a fish casserole, with potatoes, onions, tomatoes, peppers and saffron. Sometimes the fish is cooked whole, the vegetable juices being served first as a soup, then the fish and vegetables are eaten. Try some *pulpo* — better forget that it is octopus, then you will enjoy it!

Chicken (*pollo*) is usually roast (*pollo asado*) on a spit and will be served with chipped potatoes; these can often be offered as 'Take away' meals.

Desserts (*postre*) are usually fresh fruit (*fruta*), ice cream (*helados*) or *flan* which is a crème caramel. Mouth watering *gateaux* are filled with strawberries (*fresas*) and cream (*nata*).

Other island specialities are *quesadilias* — cheesecakes from El Hierro, and *rapaduras* — an almond and honey sweet from La Palma.

Our special favourite Canarian foods are:

Cobrito al horno	— roast young goat
Cochinillo asado	— roast suckling pig
Cocido canario	— Canarian stew
Cordornices rellenas	— stuffed quail
Jamón canario	— local ham
Parillada criollo	— charcoal steak
Salmonetes fritos	— fried red mullet
Atun con salsa de tomate	— tunny fish in tomato sauce
Zarzuela	— fish stew
Plátanos a la canaria	— banana fried in brandy sauce
Galletas de almendra	— almond biscuits

Drink

All the islands produce their own wine but in such small amounts that there is little for the visitor to buy. The best is said to be *vino del monte* from Gran Canaria. Lanzarote's *malvasia* or malmsey wine is in better supply; it can be bought sweet (*dulce*) or dry (*seco*). Tenerife produces a *malvasia* and a *moscatel,* El Hierro has a *vino dulce,* a sweet wine. La Palma's wine is also a *malvasia* and can be purchased sweet or dry. The latter is pleasant when chilled and served as an aperitif.

Plenty of wine is imported from mainland Spain and sells from 90 pesetas (46p) a litre. Good Spanish wines come from Rioja, Valdepenas and Jumilla. Spanish champagne costs from 250 pesetas

(£1.28) per bottle.

The local drink is rum (*ron*) which is distilled throughout the islands and sold in every bar and supermarket. It is a fiery spirit which needs to be tasted with caution. *Ron Miel* is a honey rum, similar to a liqueur. As you would expect there is a drink made from bananas: this is a yellow liqueur called *cobana*. Other liqueurs are produced from oranges, pineapples, cherries, almonds and coconuts; assorted bottles of these liqueurs make attractive souvenirs.

As liquor is duty free it is cheap; even whisky is less expensive than in Europe or at duty free shops in airports or ships. It is possible to buy English beer from a keg; however the local beer (*cerveza)* is a light cool drink which is very refreshing at all times. Mineral waters and soft drinks such as Coca-cola and Seven-up are plentiful. The latter drink can be helpful if you have a queazy tummy.

Spanish brandy (*cognac*) is said to have a less delicate flavour than French brandy. 'Soberano ' and 'Fundador' are two Spanish brandies that are 37° proof, costing about 700 pesetas (£3.60) per litre, and worth tasting. 'Sangria' is a Spanish drink, popular with tourists, that is usually served in a jug for two or more people. It is a mixture of red wine, orange juice, brandy, mineral water, slices of fruit and plenty of ice — refreshingly cool, it can be more potent than it tastes.

Bars and restaurants

In the Canary Islands, bars they never close until the last party leaves. A tip (called *propina*) is usual. The Spanish eat canapés or appetisers (called *tappas*) when they have a drink; sometimes these are quite elaborate, almost a meal. Lunch is served in restaurants between 1300 and 1500 hrs and dinner from 1930 to 2230 hrs.

It is quite in order for unaccompanied females to use cafés, bars and restaurants. Girl students often sit in a café with a coffee for an hour or so studying their books. Friends will meet at a table in the sunshine for an aperitif, drink a glass of wine, get some olives or peanuts, and no one will hasten their departure. The end of the afternoon is the time when women take a cup of chocolate and *churros* — delicious sweet fritters, freshly cooked. Black coffee is *café solo,* white coffee is *café con leche.*

Tourist offices have lists of recommended restaurants and local newspapers have plenty of advertisements. The choice of type of restaurant or bar is enormous, nowhere could a greater variety of cuisine be enjoyed. Both Tenerife and Gran Canaria have establishments of the very highest international standard. The range goes down to the very sleazy bars in the red light districts of the cities.

All restaurants in the Canary Islands must display a tourist menu of the day *(menu del dia)* at an average price of 800 pesetas (£4.12); sometimes this includes wine. The menu might be a substantial soup, grilled steak or pork chop, salad, fried potatoes, bread, ice cream or cake. Coffee is always extra. As on the continent, in the Canary Islands food and drink consumed at the bar is usually cheaper than when ordered from a waiter *(camarero)* and served at a table.

Restaurants are graded into four categories, denoted by the number of forks *(tendores)* shown. The grading reflects the price rather than the quality of the food, with four forks being the highest grade.

The best way to sample local food is to eat where the Canarians gather. Do not be shy of entering, the islanders are well used to seeing tourists about, mostly they take little notice and just get on with their own lives.

Out of town the bars and shops can be unobtrusive, often having half closed doors with maybe a faded Coca-cola sign. Once inside the service will be friendly but not inquisitive.

Both Las Palmas and Playa del Inglés have a vast number of restaurants, bars and pubs. Many are next door to one another with the same decor and type of service. Spanish bars tend to be a little cheaper. Remember that tots of spirits are at least twice the size of those served in British pubs. The Spanish always eat when they drink and they start early in the morning, too. Children and dogs are allowed in bars, indeed it is normal to see an entire family out for vino and tappas, sitting for hours chatting. In real Canarian bars you never pay for anything until you finally leave, but these days in tourist regions, because the trade is so busy, you are expected to pay when you receive your order.

The restaurants listed below are recommended by the Tourist Office and we ourselves have found them satisfactory. However, it must be remembered that both chefs and owners change frequently, and service and standards may change with them.

Some restaurants in Las Palmas

Caminito Avenida Mesa y Lopez 82. Tel: 27 88 68. Speciality grilled meats in a rustic setting. Open 1230 to 1600 and 2030 hrs until

A contrast to the tall modern buildings, this Victorian café kiosk in Parque de San Telmo provides a haven for refreshment and rest.

midnight, closed Sunday. Visa, American Express and Diners Card.
Churchill Avenida Leon y Castillo 274. Tel: 24 19 92. Located in the colonial style British Club, this restaurant is popular with Canarians as well as visitors to the island. International cuisine. Open 1330 to 1600 and 2100 hrs to midnight, closed Sunday. Visa, American Express and Master Card.
Danubio Azul Calle Sargento Llagas 37. Tel: 27 44 86. Hungarian style restaurant, speciality goulash, Hungarian wine, live Hungarian music, entertaining. Open 1800 to 0100 hrs, weekdays, 1330 to 1600 and 1900 hrs until midnight, closed on Sunday. Visa and American Express.
El Amir Calle Olof Palme 36. Tel: 22 12 43. Lebanese cuisine, also Take-Away. Open 1300 to 1700 and 2000 to 0100 hrs, closed Monday. Visa and Master Card.
El Cerdo que Rie (The Laughing Pig) Paseo de las Canteras 31. No telephone. Easily located along the Canteras seafront, in basement. Specialities grills and flambées, moderate prices. Open 1700 to 2300 hrs all week. All credit cards accepted.
El Fogan Calle Galileo 5. Tel: 26 25 63. Owned by a British couple, here is where you enjoy roast beef and Yorkshire pudding on Sundays. Fish and chips. Open daily except Monday.

El Jardín Botanico Hotel Melia Las Palmas. Calle Gomera 6. Tel: 27 76 00. A refined restaurant in a five-star hotel, with good service and beautiful upstairs view over the Canteras promenade and beach. International cuisine. Luxury prices. Open 1300 to 1600 and 2000 hrs until midnight. All credit cards accepted.

El Padrino Calle J Nazareno 1, Las Coloradas, La Isleta. Tel: 27 20 94. Speciality fresh fish and seafood, Canarian dishes at reasonable prices, good view. Open 1200 hrs to midnight. No credit cards.

House of Ming Paseo de las Canteras 30. Tel: 27 45 63. Upstairs Chinese restaurant with view of Playa Canteras, popular prices. Open every day, 1200 to 0030 hrs. Visa, American Express, Eurocard.

Kanchon Calle Sargento Llagas 7. Tel: 27 66 45. Interesting Korean restaurant with quick, polite service and good prices. Open 1230 to 1530 and 1900 to 2300 hrs, closed Sunday. No credit cards.

Kim's Steak House Calle Alfredo Jones 19. Tel: 26 40 57. Small restaurant run by English couple. International menu includes Indian curry, fair prices. Open 1230 to 1530 and 1900 to 2300 hrs, closed Sunday. Visa and Diners Card.

Mamma Tina Calle Jesus Ferrer Gimeno 10. Tel: 27 46 91. Small Italian restaurant noted for its pizzas and Italian dishes, menu of the day and good selection of desserts. Open 1300 to 1545 and 2030 to 2330 hrs, closed Sunday. Visa.

Meson El Caspio Calle JM Duran 30. Tel: 27 07 06. The first Iranian restaurant in Las Palmas, where you can enjoy Iranian caviare and champagne. Open from 1130 to 1630 and 1930 until midnight, closed Tuesday. Visa and Master Card.

O'Candil Calle Dr Miguel Rosas 9. Tel: 22 23 70. Canarian bar and restaurant, with fast friendly service, speciality fresh fish. Reasonable prices.

O Palleiro Calle Capitan Lucena 6. Tel: 27 79 19. Elegant restaurant and *tappas* bar, regional Spanish menu, speciality sea foods. Open every day from 1200 hrs until midnight. Visa.

Parilla Hotel Reina Isabel, Calle Alfredo Jones 40. Tel: 26 01 00. Eighth floor Grill Room with extensive view overlooking Canteras Beach. International menu and luxury prices. Open all week from 1300 to 1600 and 2100 hrs until midnight. Visa, American Express, Diners and Master Card.

Pasta Real Calle Secretaria Padillo 28. Tel: 26 22 67. Bistro type Italian restaurant that serves vegetarian dishes. Open daily for lunch and dinner.

Presidente Calle Barcelona 13. Tel: 24 75 85. A small quiet restaurant offering Sushi and Japanese cuisine, at reasonable prices, but not as cheap as Chinese. Open 1300 to 1600 and 1930 to 2430 hrs, closed on Sunday. American Express.

Restaurant Indio Albareda 55, Soler de España (Puerto shopping centre). No telephone. Serves genuine Indian dishes and Menu of the Day. Not expensive. Open all week, half day on Saturday and closed on Sunday. No credit cards.

Tenderete Calle Leon y Castillo 91. Tel: 24 63 50. A high class restaurant that has a famous Canarian chef. Specialities, fresh fish and Canarian cuisine. Open all week 1300 to 1700 and 2000 hrs until midnight. Visa.

Restaurants in the centre and north

Casa Miranda Camino Vecinal, Calle Los Hoyos 90, Tafira Alta. Tel: 35 45 10. Typical Canarian restaurant with good service and reasonable price, specialities pork and rabbit. Open every day from 0900 to 0100 hrs. No credit cards.

El Castillo Mirador San Bartolomé. Tel: 79 80 07. Canarian menu, speciality grilled meats, spectacular views. Open daily at 0900 hrs for breakfast.

Fragata Puerto de Sardina. Tel: 88 32 96. This fish restaurant is right by the harbour, serving Canarian dishes as well as local caught fish. Average prices.

Hao Santa Lucia. Tel: 79 80 09. A most pleasant, rustic eating place in colourful mountain village, near the Guanche Museum, speciality Canarian cooking. Garden. Open every day from 0900 to 1900 hrs. No credit cards.

Jardín Canario Carretera del Centro km7, Tafira Alta. Tel: 35 16 45. A lovely view from windows overlooking the botanical gardens. Typical Canarian food and not expensive. Open daily.

La Masia de Canarias Calle Murillo 36, Tafira Alta. Tel: 35 01 20. In a rustic setting with outside bar. This is a delightful Canarian eating place, busy at weekends. Open daily from 1300 to 1600 and 2000 hrs until midnight. Visa, American Express and Master Card.

La Taberna de Cho Zacarias Avenida Tinamar, San Mateo. No telephone. Old farmhouse setting with Canarian cuisine. Open from 1300 to 1600 hrs, closed on Monday. No credit cards.

Meson Silla Artenara. Tel: 65 81 08. Interesting setting partly in a cave and on a terrace with wide panorama. Wholesome Canarian cooking and reasonable prices. Open from 0900 hrs until dusk. No credit cards.

Princesa Guayarmina Valle de Agaete Km7 (Los Berrazales). Tel: 89 80 09. This restaurant with the same name as the two star hotel

This unusual doorway is the entrance to the Castillo Ramón restaurant in the tiny inland village of Cercado de Espino.

serves good Canarian dishes, including local fish. Not expensive. Open daily 1300 to 1500 and 1930 to 2330 hrs. No credit cards.

Restaurants in the south

Acaymo Carreterra a Mogán. Tel: 74 02 63. With a lovely terrace overlooking the valley of Mogan. Meals are prepared carefully, specialities Canarian and Italian dishes, reasonably priced. Open 1200 to 2300 hrs, closed Tuesday. Visa, Master Card and Eurocard.

Bahia Playa Porto Nova, Puerto Rico. Very good International food and inexpensive, but can be noisy.

Bar Chapperel Puerto Rico, near Commercial Centre. *Tipico* Canarian food and atmosphere, very small and quiet. Inexpensive.

Castillo Ramón Cercado de Espino. Tel: 73 62 43. Tucked away in the Barranco de Arguineguin. This attractive bar restaurant is in German style. Upstairs is a mock knight's dining hall for medieval banquets (by reservation). Donkey rides for all, music and dancing on Friday and Sunday. Open from 1000 until 2100 hrs.

Chez Mario San Agustin. Tel: 76 18 17. Mainly Italian and International dishes are served and prices reflect the quality of the good service. Open daily from 1900 to 0100 hrs. All credit cards.

Loopy's Tavern San Agustin. Tel: 76 28 92. Always busy, this rustic type restaurant is noted for its grills. Good place to take children. Open from 1000 hrs until midnight. Visa.

El Sultan Bahia Feliz, Carreteria del Sur Km44. Tel: 76 46 08. Excellent Arab and European menu, also fresh fish and good bodega. Open daily from 1900 hrs until midnight. Visa, Diners Card, American Express and Master Card.

Orient Express Commercial Centre, Puerto Rico. Upstairs good selection of mostly oriental dishes, good value.

Tu Casa Puerto de Mogán. Tel: 74 00 74. Fresh fish and meats with local grown fruits, papaya, mangoes, avocados. Prices reflect high quality. Open 1200 to 2100 hrs, closed on Tuesday.

Night life

There is plenty to do in the evenings if you are in any of the big holiday resorts and especially the capital. You will find night clubs, casinos, discos, theatres, cinemas, bingo halls, bowling alleys and flamenco shows.

It is well known that the term night club (*sala de fiesta*) means a place where a wife or girl friend can be taken without embarrassment; often it includes flamenco and folk dancing. The shows in a cabaret are usually of a less innocent character.

Las Palmas has a glittering nightlife, and provides Topless Clubs, Sex Shows and the like. A colourful evening entertainment is La Scala Gran Canaria at the **Hotel Tamarindos,** San Agustin, an international floor show that is glittering and slick, with topless show girls, ice show, singers, comedians and flamenco dancers. You sit and have dinner and then dance to a modern band before the show begins. There is a late show on Thursday, Friday and Saturday at 2330 hrs. Admission with dinner costs 6,800 pesetas (£35). There is a casino in the Hotel Tamarindos. Take your passport and wear formal dress (a tie is obligatory for men). Open from 2100 to 0400 hrs daily.

In Las Palmas, the **Hotel Santa Catalina** has a casino with roulette, black jack, baccarat, chemin de fer and slot machines. Admission costs 500 pesetas (£2.57).

Another form of evening entertainment are the many night excursions by coach. Often these start from one of the hotels and journey into the mountains to a *ranchero* for a barbecue. The inclusive price will allow for some free drinks and a generous dinner, entertainment and dancing to a live band. Singing on the coach ride home is not compulsory! Other evening excursions include visits to night clubs with tables being reserved, a free first drink and dancing between shows.

Discos

Discoteca are the usual discos with flashing lights, modern music and a small dance floor. A few have free entrance but generally it costs about 500 to 1,000 pesetas (£2.75 — £5.15), which includes the first drink; further drinks will cost the same price. Discos open about 2200 hrs and last until 0500 hrs. Popular discos are:

● Las Palmas
El Coto Hotel Melia Las Palmas.
Dino's Hotel Bardinos.
Wilson's Calle Franchy Roca 20.
Zorba's Calle Luis Morote. Admission 1,000 pesetas (£5.15).

● Playa del Inglés
Joy Avenida Gran Canaria. Good music and service.
Belle Epoque Hotel Buenos Aires. For the newest disco rhythms.
Pascha next to Hotel Rey Carlos, Avenida de Tirajana. Mixed music programme.
Spider Hotel Continental. Well established, three bars and International disco music.

● San Agustin
Beach Club Partly open air, with a swimming pool.

Bingo
Bingo is played in several hotels, including the **Hotel Imperial Playa,** Playa de las Canteras, Las Palmas. There is also **Bingo Circulo Mercantil,** Plaza de San Bernado, Las Palmas, every day at 1700 hrs. You need to take your passport.

Museums

● Las Palmas
Museu Canario (Canarian Museum) Calle Dr Verneau St 2. Tel: 31 56 00. Open from Monday to Friday from 1000 to 1300 and 1600 to 2000 hrs. Saturday and Sunday 1000 to 1300 hrs. Admission 300 pesetas (£1.54). Founded in 1879 it has an excellent collection of pre-hispanic objects belonging to the ancient inhabitants, the Guanches. The library has 40,000 volumes and is open Monday to Friday from 1600 to 2000 hrs.
Casa de Colon (Columbus House) Calle Colon 2. Tel: 31 12 55. Open Monday to Friday from 0900 to 1400 hrs, and Saturday from 0900 to 1300 hrs. Admission 50 pesetas. Collection of objects and documents relating to Christopher Columbus, also paintings and sculptures.
Casa Museo de Perez Galdos Calle Cano 33. Tel: 36 69 76. Open from 0900 to 1300 on weekdays. Admission free. A lovely old mansion with personal mementoes of the Canarian writer.
Nestor Museum Doramas Park. Tel: 24 51 35. Open Monday to Friday 1000 to 1300 and 1600 to 1900 hrs. Admission 50 pesetas. Paintings and works of Nestor de la Torre in a Canarian village.
Museum of Religious Art by the Cathedral, Calle Espiritu Santo. Open Monday to Friday from 0900 to 1400 and 1600 to 1800 hrs, Saturday 0900 to 1400 hrs. Admission 100 pesetas. Collection of valuable images, paintings, sculptures and tapestries.

● Ingenio
Museo de Piedras (Stone Museum) Las Mejias. Open from 1000 to 1300 hrs. Rambling old Canarian house and patio, with a collection of stones, crystals, quartz, birds, plants and embroidery. Souvenirs can be purchased.

● Santa Lucia
Las Fortaleza (Guanche Museum) Open every day from 1000 to

1600 hrs. Admission 100 pesetas. In an old farmhouse, a collection of ancient Guanche relics, implements and skeletons.

Art galleries

Galeries for the purpose of purchasing paintings are to be found in Las Palmas at:
Galerie Madelea Vegueta, Las Palmas (in front of the cathedral).
Mutua Guanarteme Calle Perez Leon y Castillo 57, Las Palmas.
Cueva Puntada Calle Perez Galdos 19, Las Palmas.

Concerts

A Festival of Music is held in Las Palmas, at the Perez Galdos Theatre, between October and June. The London Symphony Orchestra, Royal Philharmonic Orchestra of London, the Philharmonic Orchestra, Leningrad and the Orpheus Chamber Orchestra all give concerts. During April and May the Spring Festival of Dance has performances by world famous artistes. Opera, too, is represented with performances given during February and March in Las Palmas.

Andalusian and folk groups

Several times a week there are shows at the Casino in San Agustin. Details are to be found on hotel notice boards. There are also performances in Las Palmas at the Canarian Village, Doramas Park, on Sunday at 1145 and 1315 hrs, also on Thursday at 1730 and 1900 hrs.

Sports and pastimes

Because of the mild climate and the proximity of the sea it is possible to participate in a wide selection of sports. Good facilities are provided on the major islands. The Canarians enjoy all forms of leisure activity and keep themselves very fit.

Land sports
Archery can be enjoyed in the grounds of a number of hotels.

Billiards is played in many hotels and bars on the island; tourists are welcome.

Bowling alleys will be found in all the tourist areas and cities, often with 12 fully automatic tracks, and smaller ones in some hotels. Very popular with the Canarian youth.

Bridge clubs exist in the cities and the game is played in most hotels. The British Clubs in Las Palmas, Gran Canaria and in Puerto de la Cruz, Tenerife have keen members who welcome visitors.

Bullfights In Tenerife the bullring is on the Rambla de Generalisimo Franco in Santa Cruz. In Gran Canaria it is 4 kms south of Playa del Inglés. Travel agents and hotels display posters when bullfights take place. Admission is usually about 900 pesetas (£4.50).

Camel safari The camel is used for working in the fields for part of the day. The rest of the time he is expected to take squealing tourists for rides. Maspalomas in Gran Canaria and the Fire Mountain in Lanzarote are the best places to have your camel ride. The camels, which are technically dromedaries, have wooden seats on which two people sit, one on each side of the animal. Not for the faint hearted, for the animal gives a great lurch as it gets off its knees! The movement is pleasing provided you can relax and not knock your back against the hard seat. An exhilarating experience for the adventurous.

Canary wrestling (*lucha Canaria*). The oldest and most typical of Canary sports, with traditions rooted in early history long before the Spanish conquest. It is a carefully preserved sport which young Canarians participate in with great keenness. *Lucha Canaria* is played by two teams of twelve wrestlers (*luchadores*). A special ring of 9m diameter is used with a thick layer of sand to prevent injuries. The wrestlers go barefoot, dressed in shirt and shorts, the purpose of the fight is to floor one's adversary. Canary wrestling is incredibly popular, and boys start to learn at the age of three and carry on until about thirty five. Every town and village has a team and there is much rivalry. There are many grips and kicks to be learnt, all very technical. It is advised that visitors do not participate in this particular sport. Tourists can see the wrestling at fiesta time, and also at Lopez Socas Stadium, Las Palmas and in the village of El Tablero, near Maspalomas.

Chess (*ajedrez*) is often played in the open air; one of the best places to play or watch the game is in the Plaza Santa Catalina, Las Palmas. You can sit down and play at a chess table for as long as you like, provided you are not defeated.

Cock fighting is permitted in all the islands. In Las Palmas fights take place between December and May at the Lopez Socas Stadium, and also in Arucas. Admission is free and the event lasts for about two hours. The tourist office has details.

Donkey safari Donkeys are still used as beasts of burden in the country. Nowadays they also have to toil up mountains with excited tourists astride their backs. Visitors are taken to a ranch and allocated a suitable beast, then in convoy they trail among the cactus and palm trees. It can be a hilarious outing for all the family, with guitar music, singing and plenty to eat. Details are advertised in hotels and travel agents. (See also Chapter 4, Excursions.)

Flying Sports airfields are found in Tenerife, Gran Canaria and Lanzarote. Visitors can have the opportunity to see the islands by air. Advance booking is necessary. Aircraft like the Cherokee 180, which takes three passengers, are used. Information from Tourist Office or travel agent.

Football This game comes top of the popularity polls. In every small village a space has been cleared for a football pitch. Local teams compete in an inter-island league. The big stadiums are in Las Palmas and Santa Cruz.

Go-Karting is a very new sport to the islands. A Go-Kart centre has been constructed about 5 kms north of Playa del Inglés, Gran Canaria. Open daily from 1000 to 2300 hrs, for adults and children; there are four kinds of Kart. There is a bar-restaurant. A second centre is located on the road to the Parrot Park from Maspalomas.

Golf There can be few places where this sport is played in such original surroundings: on a volcanic crater and in a desert. Both these courses are on the island of Gran Canaria. Other courses are situated in Tenerife and Lanzarote. All clubs are open to visitors; clubs, caddies and trollies are available.

The entrance to **The Campo de Golf** (Avenida de Africa, Maspalomas. Tel: 76 25 81) is located past Playa del Inglés, before you reach Faro de Maspalomas. It is quite a feat to have created this green oasis on the edge of the sand dunes in such an arid part of the island, and only the most modern watering system could maintain the course in such good condition. April and May are recommended as the best times to play golf here. There are fewer visitors and the spring like weather is more conducive. The low lying club house includes a restaurant and snack bar. This 72 par, 18 hole course also has a two floor driving range and putting green. Open from 0800 hrs until sunset. Green fees for 18 holes, 5,500 pesetas (£28); power caddies, 4,000 pesetas (£20.60); trolleys, 400 pesetas (£2). There are hotels in the vicinity.

Spain's oldest golf club **The Royal Las Palmas Golf Club** (Carretera de Bandama Km 5, near Santa Brigida and fifteen

The Royal Las Palmas Golf Club, set on the side of the Bandama volcanic crater, is the oldest golf course in Spain.

minutes drive from Las Palmas) was founded in 1891 and holds its centenary in 1991. At the same time the Spanish Open Championship on the European circuit will be held here. The club house has interesting memorabilia of past members, golf personalities and trophies, and there's an elegant atmosphere, with a pleasant bar and restaurant and welcoming staff. The 18 hole course is Par 71 and two of the fairways have recently been lengthened. Good practice facilities include a driving range, putting green, floodlit pitch and approach practice area. Teaching pros, caddies and power trolleys are available. Since it is near the Caldera Bandama, which is 609m high, the views from the course and club house are extensive, looking over to Las Palmas, the sea and the mountains. You will need to produce proof of your handicap if you wish to enter club competitions. In the same grounds is the Bandama Golf Hotel, just 10m from the first tee. There are facilities for riding, tennis and a swimming pool.

Greyhound racing takes place at night in the Canadroma, Playa del Inglés. Admission is free and there is a bar and restaurant. The standard of racing is good. Commencing at 2000 hrs from Tuesday to Saturday, 1800 hrs on Sunday, closed on Mondays. There is an electronic betting system and an English translation explains the betting rules. There is also racing every evening at 1900 hrs in the Nuevo Campo España Dog Track, Calle Obispo Romo 1, Las Palmas. Tel: 25 06 16.

Hang gliding There are week-end flying courses, with expert tuition at: Escula Tamaran, Leon y Castillo 244, Las Palmas. The sport is also practised at Los Cristianos, Tenerife.

Ice skating There is a rink in Gran Canaria and ice skates may be hired. Palacio de Hielo, Avenida de Escaleritas 31, Las Palmas.

Keep fit classes and programmes for physical training, jogging, judo and karate are organised in some of the larger hotels, especially those run by Germans and Scandinavians who are particularly keen on physical fitness and run large sports programmes for holidaymakers.

Motor racing Sporting car racing is very popular in Gran Canaria. The El Cortes Inglés Rally in October is valid for the European Championships. The Maspalomas International Rally is second in importance. With foreign and local competitors these exciting races are watched by thousands of fans.

Mountain and hill climbing are enjoyed in Tenerife and Gran Canaria. In Gran Canaria the National Delegation of Youth organises walks and rock climbs. There are two mountain refuges and sometimes arrangements can be made to hire equipment.

National Delegation of Youth, Plaza del Cairasco, Las Palmas.

Riding There are stables at El Oasis, near Faro, Maspalomas. Open 0800 to 1800 hrs. Also camel rides. The Picardo de Club de Golf de Bandama organises horse-riding classes and excursions.

Squash Squash courts are to be found in some of the larger hotels and in Puerto Rico by the main bus stop.

Tennis is a much practised sport amongst the Canarians and tourists. Public tennis courts are part of most of the modern tourist complexes; with the warm nights many are open until late at night, being floodlit. Most large hotels have tennis courts and coaching is available. Cita Tennis Club, Avenida de Francia, Playa del Inglés. Tel: 761483; Club de Tenis de Gran Canaria, Parque Doramas, next to Hotel Santa Catalina, Las Palmas. Tel: 24 34 13 it has four courts; Club de Tenis, near Los Palmitos (the Parrot Park). Tel: 76 14 36.

Walking The Canary Islands offer a splendid variety of scenery and terrain for walking. Miles of golden sands enable barefoot exercise. Inland treks require stout shoes for much of the land is stony and very hard. Remember to take a map if you venture off well-known routes, as distances can be very deceptive, especially if one intends to climb along the gorges (*barrancos*) or over the mountains. Another warning; there is very little evening and dusk falls quickly between 1800 and 1900 hrs. Best to check with a local person before you set off on any long walk and let someone know which route you intend to go. Take some rations, a compass and a hat — it's great fun walking in the islands, if done with caution. Strongly recommended for reading is the book *Landscapes of Gran Canaria*. It gives many routes and sensible advice. (see Bibliography, Appendix D).

Sky Gliding Details can be had from the Tamarin School Club, Leon y Castillo 244, Las Palmas. At weekends they will be found on the Maspalomas Dunes.

Swimming The Canarian beaches (*playas*) offer interesting swimming all the year round with the sea temperatures never really cold. El Hierro, Gomera and La Palma are rather short of good beaches. The other four islands have a wide choice; golden sands, black sands, fine pebbles and rocky pools, always with lovely clear water. Seas are mostly calm, but remember this is the Atlantic, and big rollers can soon blow in, turning a tranquil sea into a fury of white foam and pounding breakers. Undercurrents around rocky areas can sometimes be dangerous. In tourist resorts a red flag is flown when bathing is considered unsafe by the lifeguards. Some of

The beach at Playa de las Canteras has clean golden sands, sunbeds and clear water for a safe swim.

the best beaches include Teresitas in Tenerife, Playa del Inglés in Gran Canaria, Playa de los Pocillos in Lanzarote and the wonderful stretch of almost deserted sand at Jandia in the south of Fuerteventura.

Public swimming pools are found in Las Palmas and elsewhere. All big hotels, apartment blocks and villas have outdoor pools including smaller ones for children.

Trotting horse races Races with trotting horses take place on Sundays and holidays, at the Nuevo Campo España Dog Track, which is behind the Nilo Commercial Centre in Playa del Inglés. There is also racing in Telde.

Water sports

Nautical activities abound around the island, for the warm sea temperatures greatly encourage beginners and experienced water sports people to indulge to the full.

Fishing comes naturally to Canarians who spend many hours of their spare time with a rod. Often they are contributing to the family diet. Most tourist places have jetties, harbour walls, rocks and beaches suitable for fishing. Rods, tackle and bait are for sale. Boats with rods may be hired from a number of fishing ports and villages.

Deep sea fishing The waters around the islands are noted for big game fish and every year fishermen from all over the world return to Puerto Rico for international competitions. Many record catches have been made in these waters.

Sport fishing is expensive for the demand is high. Boats are of a high standard and powerful. Great excitement is felt when around 1600 hrs each afternoon, these fast little boats return to harbour, their tough captains chewing a fat cigar with great nonchalance, while admiring tourists gasp with wonder at the huge fish. Marlin, tunny, shark, swordfish and barracuda are the big ones, with mackerel and sardines being used as bait. From Santa Catalina Pier in Las Palmas, a boat leaves every day at 1200 hrs, to go deep sea fishing, especially for sharks.

Diving The seas around the archipelago have interesting under-water volcanic rock formations. Coral barriers and marine life make sub-aqua diving and swimming a fascinating pastime. Beginners courses in sheltered harbours, and boat excursions to interesting sites, are arranged. Aquamarine, near Arguineguin, has full scale equipment for a sea film and photographic school. Cameras and lights can be rented.

Sailing Every island, except El Hierro, has a yacht club. Many Canarians own either a sailing or motor yacht. The sport is very much on the increase and new yacht marinas are being developed. Water sport schools are big business in the tourist resorts, frequent outings are arranged for all classes of sailors and beginners. The International Sailing School, Puerto Rico, speak English and welcome visitors. A number of tourists take boats by trailer to the islands, especially in the winter season. Details of sailing schools and events are advertised in hotels and the local paper. All types of boats are for hire.

Water ski schools are mostly found in the southern parts of the islands where the waters have a lower swell. Courses for beginners and more experienced water ski enthusiasts are well advertised in shops and hotels. You can water ski in Puerto Rico at the Club de Vela Cirus, where boats and canoes are for hire.

Windsurfing This fascinating sport is rapidly gaining immense popularity around the coasts. Many visitors arrive with their own boards on top of vehicles. Windsurfing can be a bit more tricky than it looks and professional advice is given on many beaches. Learning in sheltered waters helps to give confidence. This can be done at Puerto Rico. If it is all too difficult do not despair, you can always hire a *pedallo* (pedal boat) for 500 pesetas (£2.57) per hour — for two!

SIX

Practical information for visitors

Budgeting for your holiday

The cost of living should not prove higher in the Canary Islands than Europe or the UK. Generally speaking, package tour holiday-makers require spending money for entertainments, drinks and possibly additional meals, unless the package includes full board. You must allow for extra costs such as taking part in sports and excursions, the hire of chairs and sun umbrellas, laundry, and tips (*propina*) for waiters, taxi drivers and porters (about 10 per cent); and maybe some extra film for the camera and souvenirs.

Prices in tourist areas will probably be a few pesetas higher than elsewhere but if one takes into account the extra cost of travelling to a non-tourist area to do one's shopping, it will probably work out much about the same. For the independent traveller, it is possible to live quite cheaply especially by buying local foods. Chickens, tomatoes, cucumbers, eggs, bread and many drinks are less expensive than in the UK. Bars and restaurants are less costly and give a cheerful and good service.

Chemists

The Spanish for chemist is *farmacia* and they are marked by a green Maltese cross. Unlike in the UK, the chemists in Spain and the Canary Islands do not sell toiletries, only medication, but they are able to give you advice and First Aid. For toiletries you must go to a *drogeria* or *perfumeria*. In Gran Canaria chemists are to be found in all towns and tourist resorts like Playa del Inglés. Maspalomas and Puerto Rico. In general they open from 0900 to 1300 and 1630 to 2000 hrs, Monday to Friday, Saturday 0900 to 1200 hrs. As in the UK there will be a chemist open late and on Sundays and public holidays. The rota should be displayed on the doors.

Detail from the graceful frontage of the Church of San José, located a short distance inland from the Playa de las Canteras.

Church services

The Canarians are mostly Roman Catholics and have churches in all towns and villages. Visitors are always welcomed with courtesy.

Anglican and Evangelical Churches are to be found in the main tourist resorts. Lists of addresses with times of services can be obtained from Tourist Offices and large hotels. There are no synagogues in the Canary Islands.

— (Anglican) Holy Trinity Church, Calle Rafael Ramirez, Las Palmas

— (Baptist Evangelical) Ingeniero Salinas 17, Las Palmas

— (Evangelical Church) Calle Juan de la Cosa 24, Las Palmas. Tel: 26 61 59

Clothes

You will need lightweight clothes for the Canary Islands. A heavy top coat is not necessary but windcheaters, anoraks and woollen jumpers are essential when visiting high mountain areas. A lightweight raincoat may prove useful.

Generally speaking, loose-fitting cotton and drip-dry garments are the most comfortable. For walking in the hills take stout flat-heeled shoes, as the terrain can be very hard and stony. On the beach rubber flip-flop sandals are useful. Remember that one's feet tend to swell in warm weather so take light footwear.

Sunhats and sunglasses should be used, for the sun in the Canaries is strong and care must be taken to avoid sunstroke.

Evening wear is mostly casual. Some hotels and restaurants require men to wear ties and jackets. When visiting churches it is not essential to wear a hat or scarf but it is expected that you will not be wearing beach clothes. Skimpy clothing is frowned on in towns. Some banks and petrol stations will refuse to serve you if you are not adequately covered.

On beaches bikinis are permitted and topless sunbathing is seen. Notices are displayed in the few places where naturists may take off their clothes, such as Maspalomas Dunes in Gran Canaria.

Buying clothes locally

When in Tenerife, Gran Canaria and Lanzarote you will be able to purchase any clothes you may require from a good selection of shops. The main tourist resorts have plenty of boutiques with modern styles. men's and children's clothes are available, too, in all styles and sizes.

Prices cover a wide range. Many of the Paris fashion houses have shops here and the big stores have whole floors full of all types of clothing including sportswear. Bargain counters with cheaper goods will be marked *rebaja* which means a reduction in price. Sometimes the open air village markets have good bargains but examine the goods to see that they are not shop-soiled.

Being a duty free area it is possible to find oriental silks, furs and leather goods at advantageous prices. When possible it is a good idea to check on the equivalent UK price first.

The range of clothes in the shops of La Gomera, La Palma, El Hierro and Fuerteventura is more restricted. However it is possible to buy various materials and have clothes made up. In Las Palmas or Tenerife a gentleman's suit can be tailored in 24 hours.

Clothes imported from Spain can be a little more expensive. Marks and Spencer have a small branch in Las Palmas with clothes being slightly more costly than in the UK. Most of the hotels have a boutique nearby; the local supermarket will probably stock beachwear, sportswear, lightweight shoes and hats.

The local hand-embroidered blouses, skirts and shawls make attractive souvenirs. Prices vary little between the various islands.

Communications

Post

Post offices (*correos*) similar to those in the UK are in all towns and some villages. Open from 0900 to 1300 hrs. Monday to Saturday, closed on Sunday and Public Holidays.

You may have letters and parcels sent to a local post office for you to collect. They should be addressed to you (surname first, then initials) at Lista de Correos, in the appropriate town (e.g. Lista de Correos, Puerto Rico, Gran Canaria, Canary Islands, Spain). There is no charge for this service. When you collect your mail from the post office you will be required to show your passport.

In shops where you purchase postcards, stamps are usually sold as well. At the time of writing postage to the UK for a letter or postcard costs 45 pesetas (23p). All mail goes by air; parcels can be registered.

The Canary Island post boxes are painted yellow, and are similar in shape to those in the UK. The exception is at main post offices where posting boxes are in the walls of the building. Sometimes they are marked *extranjero* (for posting abroad) and *insular* (for local islands). Small yellow post boxes, square in shape may be attached to houses in remote country villages.

Telephones

Telephoning from the Canary Islands to the UK or other countries is simple, provided the coin box is not too full to accept further coins. This happens quite frequently in busy tourist centres. Look for a telephone kiosk which says *international;* those marked *urbano* are for local calls only.

You can use 100, 25 or 5 peseta coins and telephone cards costing 600 and 1200 pesetas are now available. The directions for use are displayed in several languages near the telephone. In hotels, the switchboard operator will dial your number for you and call you back as soon as the call is through. Some hotels have telephones in the bedroom. A small charge is made for this service.

When using the public telephone, first dial 07 for international calls. Wait for a high pitched continuous sound then dial the code of the country required (for UK this is 44) followed by the subscriber's code and number. In cases where the code starts with 0 it is omitted. For example, for London (071 or 081), just dial 71 or 81.

International country code numbers from the Canary Islands:-

Austria	— 43	Italy	— 39
Denmark	— 45	Portugal	— 351
Germany	— 49	Sweden	— 46
Holland	— 31	UK	— 44

The cost of ringing the UK is 110 pesetas (56p) per minute.

By dialling 9198, it is possible to arrange personal calls. *Cobro revertido* means the recipient of the call pays the cost.

For general information concerning telephones, telegrams, cables and telex, dial 003.

Telegraph

Cable messages can be passed, day or night, by way of the main telephone exchange. Dial 362000.

Telex and fax

For teleprinter service, dial 363717. For emergency remittances, one's own bank at home can send money by teleprinter to a Spanish bank. This service can be granted very quickly. If necessary, ask to use a travel agent's telex. Fax is now generally available.

Consulates

In case anything untoward should happen like losing your passport it is useful to know the whereabouts of the nearest Consul. Police Headquarters and the Town Hall (*Ayuntamiento*) will also assist. Information notices and books in hotels are handy places for finding such addresses.

British Consulate in Gran Canaria Alfredo L. Jones 33, Las Palmas. Tel: 26 25 08.

American Consulate in Gran Canaria Calle Franchy y Roca 5, Las Palmas. Tel: 27 12 59.

Dentists

Dentists (*dentista*) are fully qualified, similar to doctors. The service is good and not over expensive. Generally one can call at the surgery, without an appointment, and take one's turn. Usually your hotel reception will be able to tell where you can get dental treatment. There is a dental clinic in San Fernando (Playa del Inglés): Dr Maya, tel: 76 51 21. Also Dr Luis de la Macorra, Edificio Mercurio, 1st Floor, Avenida de Tirana, Playa del Inglés, tel: 76 31 56.

Doctors

Doctors (*medicos*) have clinics which are run in a business-like manner. In tourist resorts, there would be an English speaking receptionist. You usually get immediate attention and pay a fee of about 3000 pesetas (£15.46) for a visit or consultation. They will give you a receipt for insurance purposes. If given a prescription take it to a chemist (*farmacia*) whose sign is a green Maltese Cross.

There are also First Aid Posts (*Casa de Socorro*), which is a national service. These posts are often in the country and the buildings are marked with a red cross and a road sign.

(Opposite) *The imposing Cathedral of Santa Ana, Las Palmas. Construction began in 1497 but was not complete until the late eighteenth century.* **(overleaf)** *The prickly pear cactus grows by the roadside. Its fruit is edible — if you can get past the sharp spines.*

Spain is now part of the European Community and there are reciprocal arrangements. If you wish to take advantage of these you will need a Form E111, Certificate of Entitlement to Benefits in the EEC, obtainable from your local DHSS Office. You need to produce your Form E111 when you require medical attention.

As with dentists your hotel reception or tour operator representative should be able to tell you where you can receive medical attention.

Medical clinics are to be found in all towns and tourist resorts. Some addresses are:

Policlinica (24 hours) Avenida de España 13 (opposite Centrum) Playa del Inglés. Tel: 76 12 92.

Clinica San Agustin (24 hours) San Agustin. Tel: 76 27 03.

Clinica Santa Catalina, Las Palmas. Tel: 23 41 22.

English Hospital Las Palmas. Tel: 25 42 43.

British American Clinic Sagasta 5, Las Palmas. Tel: 27 07 51, 26 45 38 and 26 20 59.

Dr Manuel Arkuch Calle Sagasta 62, Las Palmas. Tel: 27 88 26

Ambulance Tel: 76 10 22, 24 05 23 and 24 51 57.

Duty free allowance

The duty free allowance per adult into the UK for people arriving from the Canary Islands is:
— 1 litre of spirits over 22% **or** 2 litres of sparkling wine.
— 2 litres of still table wine
— 66cc of perfume
— 250cc of toilet water
— 200 cigarettes **or** 50 cigars **or** 250g of tobacco
— gifts/goods not exceeding £32 in value

Electricity, radio and television

Electric current voltage is 220 to 225 AC, occasionally 110 to 125 AC. Plugs are the two round-pin variety.

There are local radio stations in the Canaries. The local Canary Tourist Radio broadcasts from Monday to Saturday on FM 91.8 mhz programmes in English, German and Scandinavian languages. The English programme is at 1030 hrs. It is not possible to receive this broadcast throughout the islands; at present it can be heard only in the south of Gran Canaria. The World Service of the BBC is on short wave. It is possible to hear Radio 4 on long wave when atmospheric conditions are good and, generally, when it is dark.

British television sets are not suitable in the Canary Islands. (Spanish television uses Norma G for black and white and Pall for colour.) Most hotels and many bars have black and white or colour television, and nearly all the programmes are in Spanish and relayed from mainland Spain. ITN News, in English, can be seen on the Canary Islands TV Channel 2 at 1200 hrs, Monday to Friday, for ten minutes. This is followed by a short programme of Spanish news in English.

Fire precautions

Fire precautions are observed in the Canary Islands, with public buildings and hotels being inspected for adequate fire escape equipment. Details of emergency exits are shown in each hotel room. Modern fire fighting equipment is located in all places of population.

Hairdressing

Men's barbers are called *barberia* and ladies' salons *peluqueria*. In tourist areas prices are higher than in towns. Most large hotels have their own salons and the standard is generally very good. The Canarians have particularly well groomed hair and frequently use hairdressers.

Health

There are no dangerous animals or poisonous reptiles in the Canaries, not many flies and only a few mosquitos. The spring-like weather is healthy and invigorating. Over indulgence with food and drink can cause discomfort and an upset tummy. It is wise to wash all fruits and salads before eating.

There is no shortage of medications in the Canary Islands, but if you prefer a particular British brand it is wise to take a supply with you. Tap water should not be drunk by visitors unless it is first boiled. Water considered fit for drinking is *agua potable* and unsuitable is *agua non potable*. Bottled water is quite cheap and available at supermarkets: called *agua mineral* it is either aerated (*con gas*) or still (*sin gas*).

Canary tummy is a form of sickness and diarrhoea which may last for a few days. A suitable Spanish medication for this is available from chemists. Should the complaint persist it is advisable to consult a doctor. However cases of upset tummy are not to be expected and most people find the Canary climate will make them feel years younger.

Care should be taken to avoid too much initial exposure to the sun. The wearing of sun hats and sun glasses can be helpful. Remember that the sun's rays are very much stronger here than in the UK, so allow periods of fifteen minutes exposure to direct sunlight, at first, to parts of the body not usually exposed. Make sure that plenty of sun lotion is applied. Do not wait until the skin is turning red, that may be too late.

Sunstroke can be very distressing. Symptoms are a severe headache, vomiting and much discomfort. Mild cases require a cool shaded room with plenty of liquid. ('Seven Up' is a helpful drink.) Apply calamine or similar cream to affected parts. If the skin is blistered or the symptoms are not improving, do not hesitate to consult a chemist or doctor. Hotels have the addresses and telephone numbers of the nearest doctor or clinic.

Laundry and dry cleaning

If you wish to have clothes cleaned or laundered, it is probably easier to use the services of your hotel or apartment. Maids will collect laundry and return it clean the same day, lists of charges are usually put in each room. Dry cleaners are more rare and very busy. Launderettes are only beginning to appear in the major tourist resorts.

With the warm sunshine clothes dry very quickly so drip-dry garments are practical. There are all the usual washing powders and detergents available.

Money and banks

The Canary Islands are a part of Spain and therefore the currency is the *peseta*. The coins in use are: 1, 5, 25, 50, 100, 200 and 500 pesetas. Notes are: 1000, 2000, 5000 and 10,000 pesetas.

The 'high street' banks there are the same as in Spain and have names like, Banco de Bilbao, Banco Hispano Americano, Banco de

Santander and Banco Central. Opening hours do vary slightly but generally are 0930 to 1400 hrs daily, closing at 1300 on Saturdays. Closed on Sundays and Public Holidays. Most Spanish banks accept Eurocheque cards or equivalent, and international credit cards displaying the sign. Be sure to check with your own bank whether your cheque card is valid for use in Spain (the Canary Islands). When you go to the bank you will need to take your cheque book or traveller's cheques, and your passport; they will probably wish to know where you are staying. One can also cash traveller's cheques and exchange currency in travel agents and hotels. The currency exchange rate is displayed in most banks and travel agents. At the present time it is 194 pesetas to £1, for cheques. A small commission is charged for the transaction. Our experience is that the Banco de Bilbao gives very favourable rates of exchange, accepts Eurocheque cards and credit cards, and has English speaking staff.

The larger hotels have deposit boxes or small safes for guests to lock up their valuables. Canarians generally are law abiding but in busy plazas, markets and at fiesta time beware of pickpockets.

Newspapers and books

English daily and Sunday newspapers can be purchased in cities, tourist complexes and at airports, usually a day after publication. Newspapers are about twice the UK price. English books and paperbacks are also available in these places.

Gran Canaria has a newspaper called *Canarias Tourist,* which is written with English, Dutch, German and Scandinavian translations. There are eighty pages crammed with information for the holidaymaker; it is recommended. It is published monthly, and obtainable from bookshops and supermarkets, 200 pesetas (£1.03). *The Southern Times* is published in Gran Canaria bi-monthly, in English and German and costs 200 pesetas (£1.03)

Opticians

Opticians (*optica*) provide a very good service. In towns and tourist centres they are able to test your vision, without charge, and supply the required spectacles in about 48 hours. Generally charges are lower than in the UK, with a very good choice of frames.

Police

There are several types of police in the Canary Islands and Spain. The *Guardia Civil* who wear a green uniform with a shiny black hat, are armed law enforcement officers. It is advisable not to get involved in a misunderstanding with them, they rarely admit to speaking English and have a great deal of power. The Municipal Police are the local town and village police, either in brown or dark blue uniforms. The Traffic Police, besides controlling traffic, give assistance with breakdowns and other problems. Their patrol cars are marked *Trafico Policia*. All types of police are approachable and helpful, especially the Traffic Police. To contact the Municipal Police, telephone Las Palmas 20 98 82; Playa del Inglés 76 12 48 or 76 27 03.

Problems and complaints

Complaints about accommodation should be made on official complaints forms (*hojas de reclamaciones*); tourist establishments should have these or the Tourist Office will provide them.

Usually the receptionist or the public relations representative (*relacions publico*) will be glad to sort out your query, they generally speak English. In extreme cases it may be necessary to go to the police (*policia municipal*) or the Town Hall (*Ayuntamiento*). You will find officials pleased to assist, but be patient; the Canarian way of life is not to hurry.

Public conveniences

Public conveniences are few and far between in the Canary Islands. They are marked *aseo* or *servicio, senoras* (ladies) and *caballeros* (gentlemen). Pictographs are also used. Toilets are available at petrol filling stations. It is quite permissible to use the cloakrooms of a hotel, bar or café and it is not necessary to be a customer.

Public conveniences will be found in market (*mercado*) places but they are sometimes austere. Payment for the use of a toilet is not required but it is usual to tip the attendant 25 pesetas.

Shopping and souvenirs

Shopping in the Canary Islands is very much like shopping in the UK and Europe. Even in the smaller islands there are the supermarket-type shops with prices marked on all goods. In the tourist areas the shop assistants will understand English but their knowledge of German will be even better, owing to the higher percentage of tourists coming from Germany.

Shopping baskets and trolleys are available, any personal parcels of shopping may have to be deposited at the entrance, and a numbered tag is given as a receipt. In some shops you are expected to select your own vegetables. Sometimes meat is prepacked but usually at the meats, fish, cheese and delicatessen counters you are served. You may have to take a numbered ticket for the queue.

Amongst the many good buys in the Canary Islands are embroidery, ceramics, palm leaf baskets, wood carvings, colourful costume dolls and cigars. Because the Canary Islands have free trading, certain goods (tobacco, liquor, cameras, radios and watches) can be cheaper here than in the country of origin.

All big towns and many villages have open air markets, where the atmosphere is friendly and informal. The markets are a good place to start a conversation with the Canarians, who are outgoing friendly people. When the Canarians go shopping they like to socialise; rarely do they expect to be served without having a chat.

Taking children to the Canary Islands

Taking young children to the Canary Islands presents no real problems. The Canarians are always interested in children, and indeed look after their own with much love and care.

Hotels, apartments and bungalows have cots and highchairs, sometimes at a small extra charge (cots are 300 pesetas/£1.54 per day). Play rooms and paddling pools, plus babysitting services, help to make life pleasant for all. There are plenty of toy and clothes shops, baby foods and toilet requirements.

Amusements, train rides, playgrounds, ice creams, beach equipment, all are reasonably priced. Young children are allowed into bars, cafés, restaurants and hotel lounges until late at night. Hotels have courtesy buses to convey you to the nearest beach.

However, care should be taken not to overtire young children, who easily become excited and possibly restless with the change of surroundings. New foods may not appeal but usually staff are understanding and helpful. Do not overdo the amount of fresh fruits or salads at first. Plenty of liquid to drink is sensible.

Young children often go on coach excursions and have a happy time. Do take some toys or games to amuse a toddler, for sitting in a coach will become tedious without some diversion. Use the toilet when the coach makes a stop for this purpose; drivers have to work to a schedule and it is not always possible to make emergency halts on narrow mountain roads.

With plenty of beaches and warm sea water most youngsters are completely happy. Please do not force your child into the sea; use a little encouragement to paddle or sit at the edge, it is not sensible to be 'tough' when a child is nervous of water. Making a sand castle and fetching a bucket of sea water will do a lot towards gaining confidence. Be sure to provide the child with a sun hat and protection for the skin, and do not leave him to play in the sun for too long at a time. Guard carefully against sunburn and sunstroke (see Health section).

Time

Time is the same throughout the Canary Islands, and from the end of October to the end of March, it corresponds with the UK; the rest of the year it is one hour behind.

Tipping

Tipping is expected, as in the UK and on the Continent. In bars, cafés and restaurants, even though a service charge may be added, a tip *(propina)* in the region of ten per cent is generally given, perhaps less for a drink at the bar. The Canarians and Spanish are proud and well mannered and do not make much of the subject. Porters, maids and cloak room attendants should also be tipped 25 or 50 pesetas, though porters at airports may have a fixed charge per piece of luggage. Taxi drivers expect a ten per cent tip.

Water

Water is generally scarce in the Canary Islands and particularly in Gran Canaria, Lanzarote and Fuerteventura, as there is little in the way of natural water supplies. If any it comes from private wells and reservoir catchments of water from the mountains. Tenerife is better off for water because it has the 3718m Mount Teide. The larger hotels in Gran Canaria have desalination plants and the water is safe to drink, but to be on the safe side it is recommended that you buy bottled drinking water that is sold in all supermarkets and bars. As water is so precious and costly you are asked not to waste it.

The Intrepid Traveller

During the spring and winter of 1884 a splendid Victorian lady, Mrs Oliva M. Stone, accompanied by her husband, toured all seven of the Canary Islands. Much of their travel was by donkey and camel, but at times it was on foot.

Subsequently Oliva Stone wrote a book which was published in 1887, entitled 'Tenerife and its Six Satellites'; the maps and illustrations were from photographs taken by her husband, Harris Stone. Volume two describes her journey round Gran Canaria, Lanzarote and Fuerteventura. Her book was possibly one of the earliest of the tourist guides about the Canary Islands.

It is said that this formidable lady always flew the Union Jack from her tent and she expressed the thought that the Canary Islands should belong to England!

SEVEN

The Canary Islands and the islanders

History of the Canary Islands

The Canary Islands were known to the Ancient World under various names; the Greeks called them 'The Isles of the Blessed' and Homer described them as the location of the 'Elysian Fields'. Later Herodotus writing in the fifth century BC, referred to them as 'The Garden of Hesperides' and the archipelago was generally known to the Romans as 'The Fortunate Islands'. Much of the early history of the Canary Islands is uncertain and is only partly explained in the myths and legends that tell of the first inhabitants' experiences.

It seems likely the Canaries were known to seafarers well before the Spanish colonised the islands in the fifteenth century. The Phoenicians are reputed to have collected 'orchilla', a purple dye, from the islands during their explorations along the coast of North West Africa; they used the dye to colour carpets and clothes. The Roman writer Pliny the Elder (AD 23 to 79), writes of an expedition sent by King Juba the Second of Mauritania to The Fortunate Islands about 30 BC. Pliny tells how Juba's troops found the islands deserted but with many ruins of great buildings. The soldiers saw enormous wild dogs roaming the islands, and they brought two of the animals back to the King. Afterwards the lands became known as the 'Canis Islands', *canis* being the Latin for 'dog', and in later years the 'Islands of Dogs' was corrupted to 'Canaria'. The collective name, therefore, of the Canary Islands has nothing to do with the native bird of that name but refers to these wild dogs.

The Guanche people
When the Spaniards arrived in the fifteenth century they found a primitive race akin to Stone Age people occupying the islands. How they got there and their origins still remain something of a mystery.

The Encyclopaedia Britannica records that the aboriginal inhabitants of the Canary Islands were called Guanches (*Guan* — person, *Chinet* — Tenerife, thus 'Man of Tenerife').

The Guanches, now extinct, appear from their skulls and bones to have resembled the Cro-Magnon race of the Quaternary age. It seems that they may have come from central and southern Europe via North Africa in some distant age. The characteristics of grey-blue eyes and blondish hair still persist in some of the present inhabitants. In the two islands of Tenerife and Gomera the Guanche type has been retained with more purity than in the others. No inscriptions have been found in these islands so it would seem that the Guanches did not know how to write. In all the islands, except these two, Semitic inscriptions and rock signs have been discovered. From these facts it would seem that people from the neighbourhood of Carthage and the Semitic races landed in the Canary Islands.

The Guanches lived in natural caves; they used to paint their bodies and wear garments of goatskin and vegetable fibres, some of which have been found in tombs in Gran Canaria. Necklaces of wood, bone and shells, polished battle axes, lances and clubs are to be seen on display in the various museums in the Canary Islands. Many cave dwellings still exist today in the mountains and remain in daily use, being handed down by each generation and much sought after as part of their heritage.

In Guanche times, many very old people, after bidding farewell to their families, were carried to a sepulchral cave, given a bowl of

---

Atlantis

The original inhabitants of the Canary Island, the Guanches, lived in cave dwellings in the mountains. They did not appear to have ships or any knowledge of navigation, and there has been much speculation about where they came from. Could there be a link with an age-old legend that science has never been able to prove or disprove?

The legendary island continent of Atlantis is said to have sunk into the sea some 3000 years ago, following a natural disaster. Yet perhaps it did not sink altogether, perhaps the tops of mountains remained to be seen? Any survivors of this catastrophe would have been hill and mountain inhabitants — simple and hardy people, mostly shepherds, without much knowledge. As shepherds, of course, they would have had dogs..... And when King Juba's troops came to the Canary Islands in 30BC they found many wild dogs roaming the islands.

After all, the Atlantic Ocean is probably named after Atlantis, so is it not more likely that the legendary continent would have been there, rather than in the Aegean, which is where one of the more popular theories about Atlantis is set?

milk and left to die. Guanches embalmed their bodies and 'mummies' have been found wrapped in goat and sheep skins. In districts where cave dwelling was impossible they built small round houses; their communities were ruled by a king or chief.

They worshipped gods and goddesses, the sun and moon, believed in evil spirits and venerated the rocks and the mountains. Religious festivals took precedence over wars and personal quarrels.

During the year 999 AD the Arabs landed and traded on Gran Canaria. In the thirteenth and fourteenth centuries Genoese, Majorcan, Portuguese and French navigators visited the islands and had a friendly welcome from the Guanches.

Early in the fourteenth century, Lancellotto Malocello, an Italian nobleman from Genoa, discovered Lanzarote and gave his name to the island when charting a map. Although he exploited the natives for labour he made no attempt to take over the island.

Spanish rule

When the Spanish conquered the islands during the fifteenth century, the Guanches are said to have put up heroic resistance against the invaders and many folk tales tell of the bravery of the doomed defenders, who in some instances preferred honourable suicide rather than ignominious defeat.

The conquest of the Canary Islands by the Spanish was to take nearly a century, starting in 1402. The French nobleman, Jean de Bethancourt, under the commission of the King of Spain, together with another nobleman, Gadifer de Salle, invaded Lanzarote and Fuerteventura. After much struggle they managed to subdue the islands and to a lesser extent also La Gomera and El Hierro.

Ostensibly the Spanish invasion was to spread Christianity but they also took slaves and killed many of the inhabitants who put up a noble resistance. There was much intrigue and fighting amongst the invaders themselves when taking over the islands; this included an interim Portuguese ownership of Lanzarote and Gomera but in 1470 the Portuguese ceded their rights to the Catholic Kings of Spain. Captain Juan Rejon was sent to claim the lands for Spain and stop fighting. In 1478 Juan Rejon landed in Gran Canaria with Castilian troops; after many cruel battles he was replaced by Pedro de Vera who in April 1483 took over the island for Spain.

Alonso de Lugo and his forces also fought many battles against the Guanches before their resistance was broken. The majority were killed in battle, some taken as slaves, a few were assimilated amongst the invaders. In 1492 La Palma fell, then in 1496 the final battle was fought at La Victoria de Acentejo in Tenerife, so at last the conquest was complete and the entire archipelago was incorporated into the Crown of Castile.

When in 1492 Christopher Columbus began his search for the New World, he put into Las Palmas, Gran Canaria for repairs to his ships; later he sailed on to La Gomera for water and victuals. On future voyages he returned several times to the islands, especially La Gomera, where it is reputed he was enamoured with the beautiful widow Beatriz de Bobadilla, whom he had met previously at the Spanish court.

The islands prosper

The Canaries became a useful staging post between Europe and the Americas, but were subject to attacks by pirates from many countries, including the English, Dutch and the Moors who were looking for slaves and timber. During the sixteenth and seventeenth centuries the islands began to prosper with the cultivation of the vine, the production of sugar, and ship repairs. Canary 'sack' or 'malmsey' wine was much sought after by Elizabethan sailors such as Raleigh and Drake. Records show that Thomas Nichols, a 'factor' of an English company which traded in sugar, lived in Tenerife from 1556 to 1571. He wrote a book *The Fortunate Islands,* published in London in 1583.

In 1589 Philip II of Spain created the post of Captain General of the Canaries, fortifications were built as a means of defence and protection from raiding pirates and other invaders. Many of these fortresses remain to this day and form museums of interest to the tourist. So during the following years the islands developed and prospered, but a serious challenge to Spanish sovereignty was made by the British under Lord Nelson in 1797. They were repulsed in the Battle of Santa Cruz de Tenerife, where Nelson lost an arm, one hundred and twenty-three British sailors were wounded and two hundred and twenty-six killed.

The Paisley and Little Company of London carried out a thriving business between 1770 and 1834. They exported Canarian wine and, in return, imported to the Canaries textiles, flour, tobacco and English manufactured goods. Major business houses were established by the late eighteenth century and firms like Yeowards from Liverpool and Elders and Fyffes from London both had banana and shipping trade based on the islands.

A province of Spain

In 1823 the Canary Islands were united to become a single province of Spain with its capital at Santa Cruz de Tenerife; this caused much annoyance to Gran Canaria, who thought that Las Palmas was of equal importance and deserved the title. The Law of Free Ports was passed in 1852, turning the archipelago into a duty free area and allowing the Canarians to trade with the whole world.

The British influence continued to be strong both in Santa Cruz de Tenerife and Las Palmas de Gran Canaria. Many of the roads were built by the British and, even today, there are streets in Las Palmas named after British businessmen, such as Calle Thomas Millar and Calle Alfredo Jones (of the Grand Canary Coal and Shipping Company).

In 1903 a plan was devised to divide the archipelago into two provinces and the Partido Local Canario came into being. However it took many years for this to happen. Meanwhile, although Spain remained neutral during the First World War, the drop in maritime traffic had a harmful effect on the islands. It was not until 1927 the archipelago was declared two provinces of Spain, each with its own capital and council. The provinces are:

● Western Province
Tenerife (capital, Santa Cruz de Tenerife), La Gomera, El Hierro and La Palma.

● Eastern Province
Gran Canaria (capital, Las Palmas), Fuerteventura, Lanzarote with the islets of Los Lobos, Graciosa, Montana Clara, Alegranza, Roque del Oeste and Roque del Este.

It was while serving as Military Governor of the Canary Islands in 1936 that General Franco plotted then led the anti-Socialist revolt that sparked off the Spanish Civil War, and the Canary Islands were used as a base for training the revolutionary troops.

During the Second World War, Spain and the Canaries remained neutral. After the war, as a result of the development of modern refrigeration and commercial air transport, the agricultural industries of the islands improved. Ports were enlarged to cope with modern shipping, airports were built or enlarged.

Tourism which started with a great boom at the beginning of 1970s is now a major industry and an all-the-year-round influx of sun seeking visitors has taken people away from the land to work in hotels and shops. The Canary Islands today with a population of 1,500,000 are peaceful, progressive and working hard for a stable economy.

Background to Gran Canaria

Gran Canaria still has visible links with its ancient history: the vast number of old caves and artefacts help us to build up a picture of the original primitive inhabitants, the Guanches, who must have lived here peacefully enough, warding off incursions by slaves and adventurers, until the fifteenth century.

The greatest change in the history of the island came in 1478, when Juan Rejon was charged by the Spanish Catholic king to convert the natives to Christianity.

It is said that Rejon and his soldiers landed on the tiny islet, La Isleta, at the northeast tip of Gran Canaria. Using local palms they built themselves a protective palisade around their camp, calling it Real de las Palmas (camp of the palms). Later the name was simplified to Las Palmas.

After long years of bitter fighting and heroic resistance, the island chief Doramas died in a bloody battle at Arucas.

But it was not finally conquered until 1483, and it took until 1487 for it to be incorporated into the Spanish Crown. Las Palmas became the seat of the archipelago's bishopric and the building of the Cathedral of Santa Ana was begun.

Christopher Columbus took advantage of the port on his way to the New World. The island's carpenters and craftsmen were able to do useful repairs to his ships; water and provisions were taken aboard.

Sugar canes were imported from Madeira together with vines, and these grew well in the fertile soil. Merchants and traders set up in business in the thriving port. In 1515 a Military Governor was appointed to build defensive fortifications against attacking pirates.

With the increase of trade between America and Europe, the importance of Las Palmas as a port of call became even greater. In 1778 laws promulgated freedom of trade between the Indies and the Canaries, and Las Palmas enjoyed much prosperity; and in 1852 the Law of Free Ports was passed which turned the whole archipelago into a duty free area, allowing the Canarians to trade with the whole world.

Today Las Palmas is the archipelago's industrial centre, with oil refinery, chemical, textile and tobacco factories.

Gran Canaria has the largest livestock population of all the islands; cattle, sheep, pigs and goats contribute to the economy. Enough bananas, tomatoes and cucumbers are produced for export despite the great shortage of water for cultivation.

However, in the last twenty years the tourist industry has

developed rapidly and is now an economic factor, and still on the increase.

Canarian way of life

The Canarian way of life is like that in Spain — out-going and friendly. The Canarians like to sing, play music and dance whenever possible. For no reason at all they may greet you and shake hands. To pass a Canarian you know and not greet him is an insult. It is impossible to rush Canarians into taking a decision, but given time they will be pleased to help you, particularly if you are in trouble. Should you ask the way to a place, it is quite likely that you will be taken there, or someone else will be asked to assist you.

They are a proud people who dress well, with hair neatly groomed. They do not like tourists wearing scanty clothing other than on the beaches.

Although the bars and cafés are open all day and not closed until late at night, drunkenness is very rare indeed. Thankfully, there are few cripples or beggars in the streets. Disabled people are employed to sell lottery tickets at street corners in the towns. Old people are cared for by their families.

Visitors will notice that the pace of life will seem slower, people do not rush about frantically as in North European countries. The Spanish word *manana,* meaning tomorrow, often applies — why hurry?

Communal activities are ritualised. The evening walk and gossip, called the *paseo,* is still enjoyed in every town and village, especially in the *plaza mayor* (main square). As the sun begins to set, people walk slowly up and down the streets, the air is filled with cheerful chatter. Children play in the plazas, young girls giggle with friends while at the corners stand patient lottery ticket sellers and gipsies displaying embroidered tablecloths and souvenirs. The Guardia Civil (police) in their singular black patent-leather hats pace slowly about, always in pairs, their revolvers hanging at the ready. They, too, will stop for a coffee and a chat. Young children are allowed to stay up late so that the whole family can get together in a restaurant or on a park bench. Canarians love their children very much, and are always pleased to talk about them. It is a good form of introduction if you make a pleasant remark about a child.

The islanders consider themselves to be *Canarios,* not Spaniards, whom they talk of as *Peninsulares.* The people of Gran Canaria are also known as *Canarios,* those from Fuerteventura as *Majoreros*

In the mornings in Parque Santa Catalina you can see young students playing chess. In the evenings these tables are occupied by older men.

and those from Lanzarote as *Conejos*.

Although the Spanish culture naturally has predominating influence, there are also South American, Portuguese, German and British undertones. The British community has for many years contributed to the business way of life. It is only comparatively recently with the growth of tourism that German and Scandinavian entrepreneurs have infiltrated.

The cheerful Canarians realise that tourism is an economic necessity for them, and their good-natured acceptance of hordes of foreigners is to be admired.

Language

The Canarians speak Spanish. The accent and pronunciation is slightly different in each island but for Spanish speakers there is not much problem with comprehension. Canarians generally make an effort to communicate, and many also speak English, German and French.

Nowadays English is taught as a second language in the higher grade schools. So if you have a query you are more likely to get an answer from a student than from an older person. In the smaller country villages it may be hard to find someone who understands English at all. Thus it is sensible to carry an English/Spanish dictionary and phrase book, also a local map, when seeking directions and information. (See also Appendix 'A'.)

A botanist's paradise

The Canary Islands have been called a botanist's paradise: the physical characteristics of the islands and their climate with little variation between the seasons combine to produce a diversity of environments for a variety of flora, within a relatively small area. The islands are a true Garden of Eden where dark, dense forests give way to heathers, gorses and bracken. Steep green valleys are terraced with eucalyptus, mimosa, cork trees and broom. Lush meadows harbour butterflies, dragonflies and ladybirds amongst the wild marigolds and buttercups. Oases of palm trees give shade for the cultivation of alfalfa, while cineraria and honeysuckle mingle in the hedgerows.

In the populated areas of the island, in parks and gardens, geraniums, rosy hibiscus, carnations, marigolds, nasturtiums and bougainvillea bring a riot of colour, sometimes growing wild along the verges. The poinsettia, often in double form and of various hues from deep red to pale lemon, grows into thick hedges as high as trees. The exotic strelitzia, the bird of paradise flower with its waxen blue, white and orange blossom, and birdlike shape, has now become established as the Canary Islands' symbolic flower. And one of the greatest delights of the islands is the sweet perfume of their wild aromatic plants and exotic flowers. Laburnums, honeysuckle, broom, eucalyptus, pine, many more, blend together to create a wonderful nosegay from nature.

About 1,800 different species of plants grow wild. Some have been here since the late Tertiary period: fossilised plants have been discovered, similar to those found in Mediterranean areas dating from that time. One of the last surviving trees of the Tertiary era is the *dracaena draco,* which may be called a living fossil. The tree is known as the dragon tree, or dragon's blood tree, because of the resinous secretions which, when exposed to the air, turn a dark, blood red. The one at Icod de los Vinos in Tenerife is reputed to be at least 3,000 years old. It is a weird sight, with its main thick trunk branching out into many more trunks, and a massive ridged top with spiky green leaves. The Guanches attributed magical powers to the sap of the dragon tree and thought it a cure for various ailments.

Botanical gardens and national parks

Each wave of newcomers has introduced new varieties of plants to the Canaries, and since the Middle Ages the islands have been used for acclimatising tropical plant species before taking them to colder climates. The Botanical Gardens in Gran Canaria and Tenerife contain thousands of rare exotic plants and botanical gems from all over the world, as well as endemic species, and these gardens are well worth a visit. There is much to be seen, also, in the National Parks.

Pinar de Tamadaba, in the north west of Gran Canaria, is a natural pine forest dominated by the *pinus canariensis,* with endemic botanical and ornithological species, a nature reserve which comes under the auspices of ICONA (Instituto National para la Conservación de la Naturalezo). Around the Artenara road the *cistus symphytifolius,* with its frail papery flowers and sticky leaves, and the *asphodelus microcarpus* are common species. Nearer the centre of the forest you will notice *micromeria pineolens,* the robust shrub with a large pink bloom. Wild sage and thyme help to make this pine forest even more fragrant. Roads and paths through the forest lead to a picnic area and camping ground. Permission to camp must first be obtained from the Forestry Commission Office nearby.

Apart from the national parks, the islands have numerous places where wild flowers, ferns and trees grow in great profusion. In many ways it is unfortunate that the majority of popular tourist resorts are situated in the drier and more desert-like areas. With such a variety of entertainment and golden beaches nearby, some visitors never find the time to visit the less populated, verdant areas, and they come away with a one-sided impression of the beauty of the Canary Islands.

Wildlife

The islands' fauna are less numerous than the plants, the most famous being the giant lizards of El Hierro (*lacerta simonyi*) which grow to a length of one metre. Recently thought to be extinct they have again been discovered, but their whereabouts is a guarded secret. Smaller versions of these lizards, the *tizon,* can sometimes be observed in the drier regions; they are quite harmless. There are no poisonous snakes and only a few scorpions, mosquitoes and flies. Rabbits, hares, goats, camels, donkeys and similar animals have been introduced by man.

Bird life is varied. There are over 200 species, some so well adapted to life on the islands that they can fly only short distances. There are many pigeons, partridge, quail, blackbirds, robins and sparrows. Birds of prey such as crows, vultures, buzzards, white eagles and sparrow hawks are seen frequently. To our mind one of the finest sights is to see the magnificent eagles and huge buzzards, with their out-stretched wings, flying high and free above the mountain peaks of central Gran Canaria. Perhaps disappointingly the native Canary bird (*sarinus Canaria*), which is completely yellow when domesticated, is a brownish colour with only touches of yellow in the wild, but its song is still sweet. The Tenerife chaffinch has an iridescent black and blue plumage. But perhaps the most striking bird seen is the hoopoe, whose bold black and white wing pattern, erectile crest, pink-brown plumage and long curved bill, make it instantly recognisable; its 'hoo poo poo' call carries far.

The melody of the bird song can be heard in many parks and gardens all over the islands. The national parks, too, provide ornithologists with much to observe and note.

Migrant birds use the Canary Islands, especially seabirds crossing the Atlantic. Birds from North Africa, too, visit Fuerteventura and the sandy Jandia beaches: little egrets, sandpipers and curlews search the inland saltwater pools for food.

Brilliant butterflies, dragonflies, moths and other small insects breed in the green vegetal areas of the Canaries. The cochineal insect (*coccus cacti*) is bred on the Nopal, a prickly pear type cactus, mainly in Lanzarote; it is used to make the cochineal dye which gives a red colouring to edibles like sweets, toothpaste and lipstick. Transparent-winged cicadas with their shrill chirping, fill the air with the sounds of a tropical night.

In Fuerteventura, the North African ground squirrel has become so prolific that it is now declared as a pest. Hunting is permitted on all the Canary Islands, where rabbits, partridge and wild duck abound, and on Gran Canaria there is an abundance of quail, pigeon and turtle doves. The hunting season starts in August and continues to the middle of December.

Agriculture

Two important factors influencing climate and, consequently agriculture in the Canaries are the winds, which blow in from the Atlantic and the north-east (trade-winds), and the Gulf Stream, which flows in to warm the colder Canaries currents. The winds bring clouds which, when they hit the high mountainous areas, condense to give rain. Thus, in those islands which have a central mountainous zone, we find that the northern and western parts are humid and verdant, while the southern parts, beyond the mountains, are drier and less fertile. Much less rain falls on the islands of Lanzarote and Fuerteventura because these are much flatter; besides they are nearer to the coast of Africa and are subject to hot winds blowing from the Sahara.

At one time the economy of the islands rested on the cultivation of sugar cane, but it became unprofitable; then the vine took over — Canary sack and Malvasia were as popular as Madeira — but this too failed. Sugar and wine are still produced but today the main crop is bananas. These are exported all over the world but for economic reasons the main market is Spain. Tomatoes, potatoes and cucumbers are also important exports, and various other vegetables — such as peppers, aubergines and onions — are produced for overseas markets. In recent years the export of flowers, by air, has increased: these are mainly roses, carnations and the islands' brilliant strelitzias. Cereals, salads, greens, beans, apples and pears are cultivated mostly for the local market.

Tobacco is grown, mainly in La Palma, where factories produce cigars which have a high reputation. The cigarette industry is important in both Gran Canaria and Tenerife.

The little Canary banana, *musa cavendishii,* is deliciously sweet, to be enjoyed when there. Sometimes, as with the tomato, it is difficult to purchase the ripe fruit because they are cropped when very green. One frequently encounters huge lorries carrying enormous loads of the heavy 'hands' of green bananas along narrow country roads; they can make travelling very slow.

On all the islands the country people work long and hard, often with hand tools, sometimes assisted by donkeys and camels — an incongruous sight. Modern machinery is gradually being introduced both in the field and packing shed.

Fishing industry

Fish is part of the staple diet of the islanders particularly those who live by the sea. They will often use a boat for inshore fishing during the night. In the early morning the entire family will be on the beach to help pull in the boats and assist with the catch. You can help too!

The recently built harbour at Puerto Mogan provides an attractive mooring for various pleasure craft and fishing boats.

Many Canarians are involved with sea fishing, the main catches being tuna, swordfish, mackerel and sardine, all of which are used for export and canning. The seas around are full of fish, great shoals are found in the waters that lie between Lanzarote, Fuerteventura and North Africa.

Sport fishing is popular in these waters and many world record catches have been made, especially from Puerto Rico, Gran Canaria.

National holidays

Shops and offices are closed on the following national feast or *fiesta* days. Bars, restaurants, theatres and cinemas are open, however, and public transport operates though sometimes the services are limited (as on Sundays).

January	1	— New Year's Day
	6	— Epiphany
March	19	— San José
(variable)		— Good Friday
		— Easter Monday
May	1	— Labour Day
(variable)		— Corpus Christi
(variable)		— Ascension
June	29	— San Pedro and San Pablo
July	18	— National Day
	25	— Santiago Apostal
August	15	— The Assumption
October	12	— Día de la Hispanidad
November	1	— All Saints
December	8	— Immaculate Conception
	25	— Christmas Day

In addition each city, town and village holds religious festivals and *fiestas* for its own patron saints. Christmas (*Navidad*) is celebrated with shops being decorated and there are scenes of the Nativity and the Three Wise Kings, for it is mainly a religious festival.

December 31st (*Noche Vieja*) is much enjoyed with parties, bonfires and fireworks. At midnight the New Year is heralded with the eating of twelve grapes, one at each strike of the clock, amidst great merriment and hooting of car horns and ships' sirens.

January 6th is the day for religious services, then the giving of presents — the most exciting day of the year for all children. Families dress in their best clothes and parade the streets and plazas, with the children showing off their new toys.

Fiestas and folklore

Fiestas are taken very seriously in the Canary Islands; religious services and processions are full of fervour. Visitors are always allowed to join in the procession and are made welcome if due respect is observed.

Once the religious part of the day is accomplished the fun and games start. Sport is part of the Canary way of life at all ages, and singing and dancing come naturally — even wee toddlers are encouraged to join in, whatever the hour. Folklore too is part of every fiesta and some interesting customs are still observed. For instance at the festival of **Bajada del Cristo** in Telde, Gran Canaria, an unusual statue of Christ is paraded through the streets of the town. Brought back by returning conquistadores, it was made by the Mexican Indians from maize, mixed with water into a kind of papier maché, and is still much revered.

Carnival fiestas are full of fun with beauty queens, decorated floats, many bands, drum majorettes and clowns. The larger fiestas in Las Palmas (Gran Canaria), Santa Cruz de Tenerife and La Palma are more like the carnivals of South America with elaborate costumes and masks, and fireworks and dancing continuing all night. The streets can be very crowded in the larger towns where care should be taken against pickpockets.

The floral carpets created to celebrate **Corpus Christi** (May/June) are a tremendous feat of endeavour, true works of art. These are said to have started in La Oratava, Tenerife, when an aristocratic lady laid some flowers on the cobbled street outside her house before a religious procession. People copied her, so evolved the carpet of flowers. Now intricate religious scenes and colourful floral patterns are created, using chalk patterns or metal frames which are later removed. Coloured volcanic sands, pebbles, salt and grains of cereal are used in some villages, while others use only leaves and flowers. After the religious procession has trodden over the carpets a battle of flowers creates much gaiety. You can see Floral Carpets at Las Palmas, Gran Canaria.

Bajada de la Rama on 4 August is a very nice feast, when the local people of Agaete, Gran Canaria, take their statue of the Virgen de las Nieves from the Ermita de las Nieves down to the sea at Puerto de las Nieves, in a colourful procession. After the religious ceremonies follows folk dancing and much celebration of this

At carnival time in the Canaries the entire family put on their colourful costumes and there is dancing in the streets.

important fiesta.

It is worth noting that overnight accommodation is particularly hard to find at fiesta time, so do book in advance.

Calendar of fiestas and festivals in Gran Canaria

January	5—	Cabalgata de los Reyes Magos (Las Palmas, Teror, Aguimes and Galdar)
	20—	Festival of Almond Blossom (Tejeda and Valsequillo)
February	—	Carnival (Las Palmas, Telde and Aguimes)
	—	Fiestas Turisticas de Invierno (San Agustin, Maspalomas and Playa del Inglés) specially for tourists
March/April	—	Semana Santa (Holy Week) (all island especially Las Palmas and Telde)
April	29—	Festival to commemorate the incorporation of the island with the Crown of Castile (Las Palmas)
May	—	Fiesta de San Isidro (Galdar, Teror, San Nicolas de Tolentino and Montano Cardones)
May/June	—	Corpus Christi (flower carpets) (Las Palmas and Arucas)
June	24—	Fiesta to celebrate the foundation of Las Palmas (Las Palmas, Telde and Arucas)
July	6—	Fiesta de San Isidro (Teror)
	6—	Fiesta del Albaricoque (apricots) (Fataga)
	16—	Fiesta del Carmen (Las Palmas, Galdar, San Nicolas de Tolentin)
	25—	Feast of Saint James the Apostle (San Bartolomé de Tirajana and Galdar)
August	4—	La Bajada de la Rama (Agaete) of special tourist interest
	15—	Fiesta de San Roque (Guia, Telde and Las Palmas)
	—	Last Sunday, Fiesta de la Virgen de la Cuevita (Artenara)
September	8—	Fiesta de la Virgen del Pino (all island)
	10—	Fiesta de San Nicolas (San Nicolas de Tolentino)
October	—	First Sunday, Fiesta de la Naval (Las Palmas and Santa Bridgida), celebrating the victory over Sir Francis Drake

November	— Rancho de Animas (folk music and dancing) (Teror)
December	8— Fiesta de la Cana Dulce (Arucas and Santa Lucia)
	25— Navidades (all island)
	31— Noche Vieja (all island) firework display

Canary music and dancing

The Canarians are a musical people, who love to sing and dance on every occasion. From a very early age toddlers are encouraged to make music; visitors to the islands are charmed to see tiny children who clap their hands and sing to a natural rhythm while at play.

Each island has its own folk dances and songs, but the general influence is Spanish and South American. The flute and tambourine are popular but the islands' most typical instrument is the *timple*. Much like a small guitar or ukelele, the *timple* was first made at Teguise in Lanzarote where there are still craftsmen making this delightful instrument.

Canary folk song and dances have a typical swaying movement, with languid drawn out melodies; gestures and brightly coloured costumes combine to make a unique and exotic impression. The *folia* is slow, the man demonstrating his feelings for the woman with dignity and restraint. *Folia* songs have been compared with the Portuguese *fado*. The *isa* is a light and gay dance similar to an English country dance.

The costumes worn by men and women are highly decorative. The women wear bright coloured, often striped, skirts over long white petticoats; sometimes the overskirts are delicately embroidered and looped up. Dainty lace-trimmed aprons and embroidered waistcoats fit neatly over white blouses with large puff sleeves. Black ankle boots, scarves and hat complete the picture. It is the type of hat which helps to identify the islander: in the eastern islands, the scarf covers the face more and the hat is wider brimmed. In Tenerife and La Palma the hat is tilted towards the back of the head.

The men's costumes include white shirts, black knee length trousers over white underbreeches, long red waistcoats and colourful cummerbunds or sashes. Woollen knee-length socks and white spats over black shoes are worn and a soft black felt hat. Sometimes a thick cape completes the costume.

Students from various Spanish universities can frequently be seen in carnival costume, singing and playing in bars, restaurants and plazas to collect money for charity.

At fiesta time glittering masks are sold, and everyone delights in dressing up. Young girls paint their faces and nails, flashing smiles in all directions, and young men wear flowing capes and carry guitars.

Exhibitions and galas of Canarian music and folk dancing are held regularly on all the islands, throughout the year. Some are planned for the tourist, but most are for the delight of the happy Canarians, whose greatest pleasure is to make music and dance.

The burial of the sardine

This important event always takes place on Shrove Tuesday, it being a celebration of the end of Carnival and the beginning of Lent.

A huge silvery, mock sardine (a symbol of the islands), about six metres long, is carried on a platform on the shoulders of eight youths, through the streets at night. Accompanying it is a children's band and a procession of 'wailing mourners', all dressed in widows' weeds: males and females with black hats, veils and high heeled shoes sob and shriek their way along, cheered on by clapping and laughing crowds. Every now and then the Sardine is tossed in the air, having a final fling before being taken on to the beach!

There a mock funeral service is conducted amid much moaning and groaning from the mourners. Finally the Sardine is set alight in a huge bonfire, which is followed by a wonderful firework display.

So ends this night of fun and frivolity — it is a great and important Canarian spectacle.

Handicrafts

All the islands retain many craftsmen and women, in some instances their skills are unique. Craftsmanship has played an important part in architecture as can be seen in the old Canary houses and churches. Implements like yokes and ploughs, kitchen utensils, beautiful looms for weaving, furniture, cedar chests and pipes for smoking, all have over the years been carefully carved from the many different types of wood growing locally. Musical instruments, too, like the Canarian guitar (*timple*) and castanets (*chacaras*) are still being made by traditional methods. The typical Canary **basketwork** has its origin in its use for agriculture.

Vara (twig) basketwork is very sturdy; made from strips of young wood like chestnut, in La Palma it reaches an outstanding quality, whilst in Tenerife it is executed with darker, wider and thicker strips of wood.

Cana (cane) basketwork can be pure cane for making delicate baskets, or a mixture of cane and twig for strength. *Palanqueta,* where strips are obtained from the stalks of bunches of dates, gives a highly decorative effect. Very sturdy baskets are made on the island of Hierro, especially at Sabinosa.

Other basketwork produces hats, mats and handbags made from the palm leaf. The central stem of the palm, the *purgano* can be used for fans and brooms. In Ingenio, Gran Canaria another strong basket is made from reeds. Straw can be used on its own or tied with bramble, to make hampers and containers for dried fruit. Each island keeps to its own traditional work.

There is renewed interest amongst the young in the ancient arts, especially amongst potters who work alongside the old crafts people. The main characteristics of typical Canary **pottery** is its simplicity and non use of the wheel, the craftsman's hands being the only means of lifting and rotating the clay. A small amount of sand is put under the clay to stop it adhering to the ground or bench.

It is fascinating to watch the work of someone like Dona Guadalupe Nubla, in the village of Chipude tucked away in the craggy mountains of Gomera. The shapes of the pots remain the same as in Guanche times.

In Lanzarote there is a famous potter, Dona Dorotea, a wonderful old lady of ninety years who lives in the north near Muñique. She has been making pottery since she was a girl and was taught by her mother, who was, in turn taught by her mother, using a primitive form of art. The clay is brought from the nearby cliffs of Famara. She works in a simple shed and forms the figures with her hands, without any form of wheel. The work is then dried in the sun and later baked on a metal frame over a fire of twigs and small corncobs. Each piece of work is signed and no two pieces are identical.

Yet another form of the art is created by Juan Brito, whose style is more abstract. In La Palma, the Benahorita people (the ancient inhabitants) bequeathed a unique type of pottery which has a wonderful glaze, and is marked with prehistoric spirals and geometrical designs. It can be purchased at Mazo and in Santa Cruz de la Palma. In Gran Canaria, pottery is made in Galdar.

Weaving is still worked on handlooms. Traditional *traperas* rugs, made from rags, are sometimes now woven with wool. Always in bright colours, they make lovely souvenir presents. Among the places where you can see this work done is the *artesania* (craftshop) near Hermigua in Gomera. At El Paso in La Palma you can find a unique example of silk weaving.

It is also in La Palma that wonderful silk shawls are delicately **hand embroidered.** The *bordados* tablecloths of La Palma are of such a high standard of craft that they are considered amongst the finest work of the islands. Although expensive to purchase they make magnificent heirlooms.

The handicraft that tourists can most easily observe and purchase is **open threadwork** (*calados*). The work is done mainly in Tenerife, Gran Canaria and Fuerteventura, but it is a cottage industry pursued when conditions do not allow work in the fields. *Calados* is executed by stretching the cloth on a frame, and drawing the threads together to form an intricate pattern. Usually each piece is worked by more than one person. Each island has its own designs and it is interesting to compare these. The same patterns appear on the blouses and skirts worn by the folk dancers.

Various schools of needlework throughout the islands are now open to visitors and the articles sold there are usually a little less expensive than in the shops. Seeing pretty young twelve-year-olds patiently working their needle must surely make you reach for your purse to keep alive the art of hand embroidery. There is a School of Embroidery at Ingenio, in Gran Canaria.

In Guía, Gran Canaria, the town is noted for its handicrafts such as ceramics, knives with carved handles and a famous cheese called *queso de flor,* which is made by curdling a mixture of goat, sheep and cows' milk, then mixing it with the wild cardon or thistle (hence flower cheese).

The list of handicrafts of the islands is long, and one must mention a few more: delicate lace work done by the convent sisters, rag dolls dressed in typical costume, woollen shawls, native clay figures, polished volcanic stones. (The *peridot* is a green semi precious stone which is made into attractive jewellery.)

Thanks to the patience of the islanders and the support of many tourists, the traditional skills of handicrafts are being preserved.

The tall circular Sol Los Bardinos Hotel overlooks the fountains of Parque Santa Catalina. This main square is a useful meeting place.

EIGHT

Las Palmas, the capital

For some the name Las Palmas evokes pictures of cruise liners and tropical islands, but in fact Las Palmas is not in the tropics, and its climate is not always as perfect as many expect. Often clouds descend from the mountains to mix with the warm air currents and create a humidity that can be oppressive. Nevertheless thousands of tourists from all over the world pour into the city.

Las Palmas is a vast and colourful city. In a way it is three cities in one: there is the old city, the Vegueta, full of historic buildings and a maze of narrow streets; then there is the smart Garden City, south of Alcaravaneras, spacious with huge office and apartment skyscrapers; and finally there is the enormous port and golden Canteras beach. Holidaymakers usually stay in hotels in the latter area. It is a good choice for those who like to combine a beach vacation with the delights of a major city. Within easy walking distance you find just about everything you need: there's a fantastic selection of shops, bars, restaurants, discos and sex shows, and there's the long promenade if you just wish to stroll. It is somewhat faded in places and distinctly grubby down some alleyways, yet Las Palmas has an exotic attraction for those who enjoy mingling amongst the many peoples of the world.

The combination of busy port with ancient and modern city makes Las Palmas a centre of international importance. Huge docks and harbour walls protect the shipping in the Puerto de la Luz where, day and night, there is activity among cargo and passenger ships. Fishing boats, too, jostle for a berth alongside the quays. The jetfoil from Tenerife and ships of the Trasmediterranea Company draw up alongside the Muelle de Santa Catalina, from where it is but a short distance to the centre of the city. A newly erected

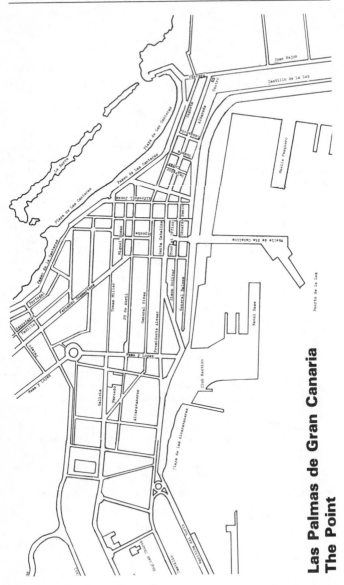

Las Palmas de Gran Canaria
The Point

terminal building has a booking office, parking and clean toilets. Taxis meet all ships. Those arriving by sea have a good view of the wide expanse of the city which has developed behind the bustling port — the round tower of the modern Hotel Los Bardineros making a distinctive landmark.

The port and its environs

The Castillo de la Luz is one of the outstanding features of the port area. It is the oldest historic monument in Las Palmas, originally a fortress built in 1494 and recently restored.

As one leaves the Muelle de Santa Catalina, still inside the dock area, there is a shop called Sovhispan, mainly for the benefit of visiting Russian sailors, selling a variety of Russian goods including genuine Russian vodka.

Outside the main docks area a short distance to the south is the Naval Dock, with its impressive walled entrance always heavily guarded. Opposite the Muelle, across the traffic lights, is the Parque de Santa Catalina, the hub of the modern city. This is not so much a park as a plaza, with tables and chairs set out on the wide pavements. Always thronging with life, night and day, it is a great meeting place for people from all over the world. Open air cafés, stalls and bazaars welcome the tourists. Goods from Africa, the Orient, Spain, China and the Americas can be found in a wonderful, colourful jumble. Portrait painters, shoe-shiners, fruitsellers, entertainers and chess players are just some of the features of this ever moving scene. Beware if you are offered a 'gold' watch, and if you are tempted to buy an embroidered tablecloth from a pretty girl you should finally expect to pay only about half the asking price. This is a splendid place to sit in the sun with your coffee, beer or brandy just watching the world go by. Try to see it at night under a moonlit starry sky, when the warm air is full of different aromas, and tall waving palms and coloured lights make a brilliant background to the animated, cosmopolitan scene.

The Tourist Office is situated in the Parque de Santa Catalina, easily identified by its attractive, low Canarian style building with dark wooden balcony. Inside you will find an attentive staff, who can provide a list of accommodation in all price ranges, a map of the city and details of bus services. The office is open from 0900 to 1330 hrs and from 1700 to 1900 hrs. Saturday from 0900 to 1330 hrs, closed on Sundays and public holidays.

Las Palmas streets are always busy with shoppers looking for tax free bargains. You will find plenty of restaurants and bars.

A shopping expedition

Shopping is delightfully easy in Gran Canaria. Las Palmas, one of the largest free ports in the world, can provide almost every need — but do not expect everything to be exceptionally cheap — prices are generally levelling off all over Europe, and in the Canaries too. Shops are open from 0900 to 1300 hrs and 1600 to 2000 hrs, closed on Sundays and public holidays. The greatest reductions are to be found in the prices of cigarettes, alcohol, radios, watches, perfumes and electrical goods. Some shops have fixed prices, particularly those run by Canarians; in others you are expected to barter — Indian and African salesmen expect this — which is a slow method of shopping, reducing the price by mutual consent.

Supermarkets are everywhere in Gran Canaria. Even the smallest village will have a shop where foods on the shelves are priced and baskets and trolleys are available. Generally speaking, most shopkeepers understand English and will be helpful, often going out of their way to assist you.

The best souvenirs typical of the island are the hand-embroidered tablecloths made in a drawn-thread work called *calados*. In these days of machine-made goods opportunities to obtain such work are rare. Costume dolls, wooden ornaments and shawls are attractive buys. Gold, silver, ivory carvings, jade, fine furs and silks are moderately priced. Goods imported from Spain tend to be a little more expensive due to transport costs. Fresh fruit and vegetables are on sale in open air markets, usually once a week. In Las Palmas a covered market, open from Monday to Saturday, is to be found in the old part of the town, the Vegueta.

The two major department stores of Las Palmas, El Cortes del Inglés and Galerias Preciados, can be found, on opposite sides of the road, along Avenida de José Mesa y Lopez north of the Alcaravaneras beach. Similar in layout, they are splendidly modern with six floors plus basement, and complete with escalators. Services offered are interpreters, currency exchange, cafeteria, restaurant, gift shop, home delivery and undercover parking. American Express, Access, Visa and Eurocheques are accepted. The basement of El Cortes del Inglés houses a large supermarket selling fresh bread, cakes, meat and vegetables. Almost next door to this store is a small branch of Marks and Spencer. However, the main shopping area of Las Palmas is around the Calle Mayor de Triana (see City tour 2, below). It is worth going to the streets where the Canarians themselves do their shopping, away from the tourist areas, as prices are sometimes more moderate. Prices in the south of the island are generally higher than in Las Palmas.

It may be of interest to you that in Las Palmas you can have a suit made in less than one week and new spectacles can be ready in forty-eight hours.

The beaches

From the Parque de Santa Catalina it is a comfortable ten-minute walk due north, along the Calle de Luis Morote to the **Playa de las Canteras.** On the way you will pass a conglomeration of shops selling a variety of goods. The Canteras beach is rated among the world's top ten beaches — so the local people will tell you with pride! Its two and a half kilometres of golden sand can be enjoyed all the year round. Protected by **La Barra,** a natural barrier of rocks out at sea, the waters are usually calm, warm and safe for bathing. At night the long, tiled promenade is a blaze of colourful lights which reflects on the waters. The evening *paseo* (walk about) takes place here, enjoyed by local Canarians as well as holidaymakers, for the Canteras beach is close both to the centre of Las Palmas and the port — the distance between the west and east coasts is only 300m at its narrowest part.

Las Palmas has a second big beach, not quite as long as Canteras, on the east coast running south of the port. The **Playa de las Alcaravaneras** is much used by the Canarians themselves and the waters are kept clean by an ingenious method of stringing a line of cork logs across the sea, so keeping the debris away from the beach.

Eating places

In Las Palmas you will find a wide range of eating places from simple Canarian bars to the grill room of a five-star hotel. Self-service restaurants are of a high standard. On your return from Canteras beach, for instance, you may wish to stop for a meal. Halfway along Calle Luis Morote turn left into Calle Tomás Miller and at No. 67 you will see a large sign 'International Self Service'. The upstairs restaurant here provides a real feast of food. For the price of 900 pesetas (£4.63) per person you may choose from at least thirty-five different dishes, eating as much as you please. Laid out attractively, the food is well cooked and good value. Drinks are extra and reasonably priced: half a litre of wine 230 pesetas (£1.18), minerals 75 pesetas (38p). There is often a Canarian folk group playing here making a collection for charity. Open 1200 to 2300 hrs. Similar self-service restaurants are to be found in the vicinity.

You will find restaurants catering for all nationalities and tastes: Hungarian, Korean, Lebanese, Chinese, South American, Indian, Japanese, Russian, German, Dutch, French, Belgian, Swiss and Scandinavian, not forgetting English and American Steakhouses. Most establishments display the menu and prices outside, in several languages.

Transport and excursions

Should you feel tired after shopping, use one of the many taxis that park outside the stores. In the city, metered travel costs are low (though if you are going outside the city limits, it is wise to agree the price of the journey before you start) — for example, from El Cortes del Inglés (department store) to the Muelle de Santa Catalina will cost about 200 pesetas (£1.00).

It is advisable to use a city bus when travelling between the old and new parts of Las Palmas. The main bus station in the old part is on Calle Rafael Cabrera, below Parque de San Telmo and between a street called Calle Mayor de Triana and the sea. In the new city the central stopping place for buses is in the Parque de Santa Catalina.

Buses are not expensive and are frequent between 0800 and 2000 hrs, timetables are available from the Tourist Office. There are three main bus routes covering Las Palmas:

No. 1   From the main bus station at Parque de San Telmo via Leon y Castillo and Parque de Santa Catalina to the port.

No. 2   From the main bus station at Parque de San Telmo to the Cathedral and Market via Tomás Morales and Plaza Cairasco.

No. 3   From the main bus station at Parque de San Telmo up the hill, past the dog racing track, Nueve Campo España, via Paseo de Chil at the back of the city to Escaleritas and the port.

In fact, one of the best ways to view Las Palmas is to take the No. 3 bus, a taxi or car along the Paseo de Chil. This long road runs parallel with the Avenida Maritima on the sea front but climbs higher up above the city, winding about to give fine views of Escaleritas, the modern part of the city, and the harbour below. Alternatively, coach tour operators have regular excursions, which can be booked at hotels or travel agents. Tours vary from half-day shopping trips to full-day excursions to visit all the main sights in Las Palmas; the latter include lunch.

From the Parque de Santa Catalina one can make a trip in a horse-drawn carriage (*tartanas*) through the city of Las Palmas. It takes about an hour, and is a leisurely way to see the sights (arrange the price first).

City tour 1
(Vegueta, the old city — Catedral de Santa Ana — Museo Canario — Casa de Colon — Mercado Municipal: half day, walking)

Visitors who come and go without exploring the old city will only half know Las Palmas, for the Vegueta, as it is called, is full of history, with its narrow streets and old buildings. The towers of the **Cathedral of Santa Ana,** founded in the fifteenth century, seem to dominate the Vegueta. Viewed from the Plaza de Santa Ana the Cathedral is mighty in appearance. The present building, begun in the late eighteenth century, is still unfinished but there is plenty to admire and enjoy. The Gothic interior soars high in beautiful deep arches, three central naves being the same height. Numerous rich relics are preserved here, including the Pendon de la Conquista (Banner of Conquest) embroidered by Queen Isabella during the conquest, but sadly, today, they have to be kept locked away, to be displayed only on special occasions.

In the palm lined Plaza de Santa Ana are statues of huge dogs representing the aboriginal dogs from which Grand Canary and the Canary Islands took their names (*canis* being the Latin for dog). This Plaza is the scene of the celebration of the feast of Corpus Christi in June when the streets of the city are richly decorated with carpets of beautiful flowers and grasses, a laborious and loving work of art. A great procession leaves the Cathedral, its huge bells tolling as the great *Monstrance* (Holy Image) is held high by six men, followed by the Bishop and Church dignitaries. Flower petals rain down from the balconies above and the air is filled with sweet perfume as the procession walks over the wonderful floral carpets. Later flaming torches lead the procession back to the Cathedral and a battle of flowers and other festivities go on long into the night.

The Plaza is always full of tourists and Canarians busy with their cameras, and with well-fed pigeons fluttering around. On the left, as one faces the Cathedral, is the Palacio Episcopal (Bishop's Palace) and at the far end of the Plaza is the large town hall.

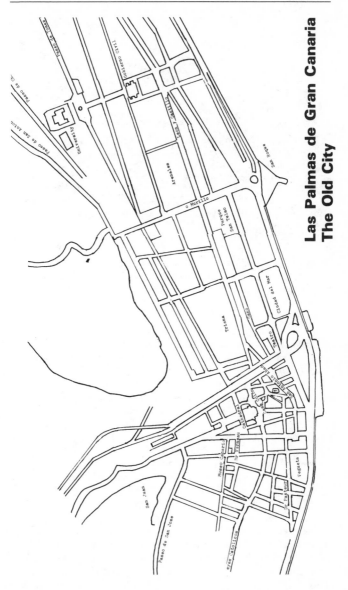

Las Palmas de Gran Canaria
The Old City

Close to the Cathedral Santa Ana are many fine old buildings, including the House of Christopher Columbus. Nearby is the small church where he prayed before sailing to America.

Nearby, on the corner of Calle Doctor Chil and Calle Doctor Vernau is the **Museo Canario** (Canary Museum). (Open from 1000 to 1300 hrs and 1500 to 1800 hrs, Saturday 1000 to 1200 hrs.) This is the most important museum on the island, and its excellent catalogue explains its purpose. The collection is divided into three sections displaying the geology, the history and pre-history of the island. The latter includes a large collection of Cro-Magnon relics, including lumps of solidified lava hurled out from volcanoes. There are even Guanche mummies, skulls and bones, and beautiful ceramics and objects from Guanche times. There are many books and maps relating to the resistance of the heroic Guanches; the museum library contains 30,000 books on all subjects.

Turning left off Calle Doctor Chil into Plaza del Pilar Nuevo one reaches **Casa Museo de Colon** (House of Columbus) in Calle Colon. This fine fifteenth century building was the military governor's house, where Christopher Columbus stayed when he visited Las Palmas. Now restored, it is a pleasing museum to Columbus and the days of the Conquest. A cool galleried patio has an old well in the centre, with hanging ferns and potted plants. Upstairs the rooms are furnished with antiques and old tapestries, and paintings hang on walls, some on loan from the Prado in Madrid.

Outside all is very quiet and peaceful. The narrow road which is still cobbled, leads to Iglesia San Antonio Abad, a tiny church built in 1892 on the site of the church where Columbus prayed before he set sail for the New World. Today beautiful bougainvillea at one side of the church climbs over the roof, a much photographed splash of colour.

In the same area, a short walk south from the Iglesia San Antonio Abad, the city's principal market lies close to the waterfront (the main Autopista to the south passes between the market and the sea). The **Mercado Municipal** is nicknamed 'The Market of the Forty Thieves' because there are that number of stalls!

Couriers from the coach excursion warn tourists to watch their pockets and handbags, so maybe the nickname is apt. Fresh fruit, vegetables, meat, fish, household and leather goods contribute to a colourful display. One of the best buys is the *queso blanco* (goat's cheese).

City tour 2
(Triana — Parque Doramas — Pueblo Canario — Ciudad Jardin — Parque de Santa Catalina: half day, walking)

Across from the market the busy highway over the Barranco de Guiniguada leads to the district called Triana. One of the first buildings you will notice is the theatre, Teatro Perez Galdos in Calle Lentini I. Built in 1919, it was decorated by Nestor de la Torre, the Canarian painter and sculptor who has done so much to promote the traditional Canarian style. Inside, the huge foyer is decorated with paintings of Canary fruits, the theme of the magnificently carved balustrades. Ballet, orchestral concerts and operas are performed during the winter.

Calle Mayor de Triana runs through the heart of the main shopping centre. From Triana, at the Parque de Cervantes, this road joins with Calle Leon y Castillo. It is along this route, about two kilometres north, that the lovely **Parque Doramas** is located. This large park encloses the Santa Catalina Hotel and the **Pueblo Canario,** a model Canary Island village. The five-star eighteenth century Santa Catalina Hotel, recently refurbished, has a luxurious setting of palms and exotic shrubs. Used by visiting heads of state its gracious interior is dignified and quiet.

Pueblo Canario is a reconstruction of a Canary village, built in memory of Nestor de la Torre, (1888-1938). The small Nestor Museum contains a collection of his works. Around a central patio, tables and chairs are set out where visitors may watch exhibitions of

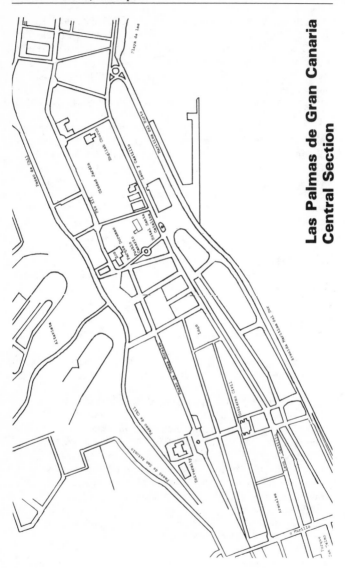

**Las Palmas de Gran Canaria
Central Section**

Canarian folk dancing and singing. Small shops selling antiques and works of local crafts people are built into alcoves around the edge of the patio. In February and March the jacaranda trees make a wonderful show with their bluish purple blossoms.

Amongst the tall palm trees and green vegetation many native specimens grow, including one of the famous dragon trees (*drago*) venerated by the Guanches. This tree looks like a relic from ancient times: the thick trunk broadens out into several massive trunks, the top being ridged with short green spiky leaves. It is sometimes called the 'dragon's blood tree', for the resinous secretions turn dark red, like blood. The park contains a small zoo, public swimming pool and tennis courts.

To one side of the Plaza de la Caleta is the Ermita de Santa Catalina, a little church dedicated to the patron saint of Majorca in the Balearic Islands, built by Mallorquin monks in the fifteenth century. It was one of the first churches to be built on the island. Look for it south of the Hotel Santa Catalina.

From Parque Doramas the Calle Leon y Castillo, continues north through the wealthy residential quarter of **Ciudad Jardin** (garden city). Large houses with pretty gardens eventually give way to blocks of recently built flats as the road leads back to the **Parque de Santa Catalina** and the port area.

This graceful figure — one of several fine statues in the Vegueta area — stands close to the Calle Mayor de Triana.

NINE

The north-east

Touring the island

The tours which follow commenced in the north, going from Las Palmas, the capital, in a clockwise direction around the island; but it is possible to start the drives from any of the southern tourist regions. Traffic though heavy, moves fast along the Autopista. For the rest of the coastline and on inland routes, the rate of progress will be about twenty five miles per hour, if that. This is because most of the roads are narrow and undulating with sharp, tortuous bends. However this should not deter you from enjoying the tours as they are all in splendid scenery (except along the Autopista).

Of recent years many roads have been widened with passing places and the majority have guard rails. However, some of the mountainous ways have very sheer drops and may cause anxiety for a nervous person. The best time of the year to see the countryside is between February for almond blossom and March and April for wild flowers. It is possible to drive round the perimeter of the island in about six hours, allowing only very short stops. Note that there is no petrol station between the Mogan junction and San Nicolás de Tolentino (38km) or between San Nicolás and Agaete (42km), and most are shut on Sundays, public holidays and *fiestas*. Remember, too, that darkness falls quickly with little twilight.

The tremendous variety of scenery is constantly changing from Atlantic views to deep ravines, then stretches of waving banana plantations, leading to rocky mountain crags and pretty rural villages. The aroma of the thick sweet pine and eucalyptus forests gives way to volcanic brooding landscapes, miradors with panoramas looking over quiet beaches and sand dunes. All this can be enjoyed when touring. We suggest you go with sun hat, sun glasses, windcheater, water and a good road map.

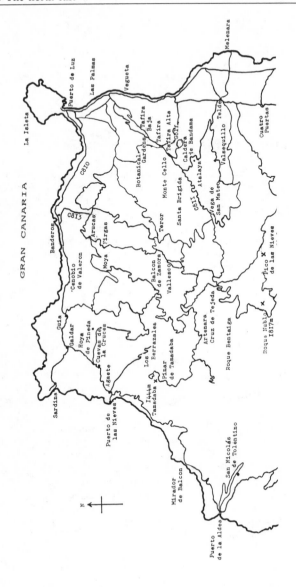

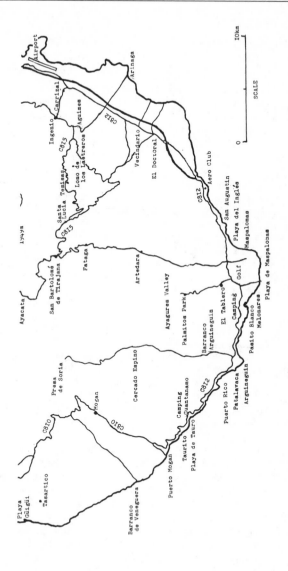

Island tour 1

**Las Palmas — Telde — Aeropuerto de Gando — Carrizal —
Ingenio — Agüimes — Lomo de los Letreros — Arinaga —
Vecindario — El Doctoral — San Agustin: about 90 km**

Most visitors to Gran Canaria tour in a clockwise direction. This is
probably because they are in a hurry to see the warmer part of the
island which is in the south.

The southern exit route from Las Palmas is well signposted from
the outskirts of the city. If you are in the centre of town, make for
the seafront and Avenida Maritima, pass the Naval Base and the
Real Club Náutico de Gran Canaria (the yacht club) and head
south. The traffic moves fast in a three-lane rush for a few
kilometres, following very close to the sea, giving clear views of the
harbour. Near the sixteenth century fortress of San Cristobel, where
old fishermen's houses are seen at the water's edge, the road
narrows, then turns into the motorway, Autopista Sud. From the
road along here, at weekends and on public holidays, you are likely
to see many energetic young Canarians, in the sea, riding the waves
on surfboards. Some are amazingly agile and leap about the waves
as if dancing; a most arresting sight.

Travel on the Autopista is fast and rather dull, for the land is dry
and featureless except for the cacti that thrive in the arid volcanic
soil. On the sea side of the road a few small clusters of houses are
to be seen along dusty roads.

Driving past the huge UNELCO electricity and desalination
installations, you will need to close your car windows as the fumes
from the tall chimneys are unpleasant and must add to the pollution
problem of Las Palmas.

A turning inland towards Jinamar leads to **Telde,** an industrial
town of importance where a great number of Canarians live who
work in Las Palmas. Many factories provide work and help the
island economy. Textiles, furniture, engineering, chemical and fish
canning works are to be seen on industrial estates. Banana packing
stations and areas cultivated with cucumbers under plastic
greenhouses add nothing to the beauty of the landscape. Telde has
not succumbed to the tourist and goes about its daily business with
very few visitors along the streets. Only the more venturesome and
thrifty will visit the weekly outdoor market to find goods much
cheaper than in the coastal towns. The parish church of San Juan
Bautiste dates from the fifteenth century. It contains a beautiful
Flemish reredos. The figure of Christ over the high altar is said to
be the work of Tabasco Indians.

Telde was the ancient Court of Doramas, the legendary native king, and today it is the island's second most important town. Driving in Telde is far from easy and parking, as elsewhere in the bigger towns, is a real problem. However the municipal police (often women) are patient and helpful. Los Llanos is the district where the Moors and slaves lived, who in the past worked on the sugar plantations.

So far your view of Gran Canaria will have been of a rather dreary and dusty landscape. It is necessary to look further inland, to where the high range of central mountains form distant peaks of reddish brown, to find real beauty in this desert like countryside. About five kilometres from Telde is the site of an old Guanche cave, Cuatro Puertas (four doors). The cave has four openings which lead into a large central cavern, which it is believed was used as a council chamber by the Guanches. The east face of the mountain is honeycombed with caves once used by the Guanches as burial chambers.

Rejoining the Autopista, roads turn seawards to the fishing villages of **La Estralla** and **Melenera**. At **Playa del Hombre** a small *urbanización,* mainly for Scandinavians, mingles with the Canarian population. These playas are being developed with modern apartments and shops used mainly by Canarians.

Nineteen kilometres south of Las Palmas and clearly signposted is the turn-off for the **Aeropuerto de Gando.** As you drive south there is a good view of aircraft landing and taking off.

The Autopista continues on past the airport for only 20 km; the road then splits into two almost parallel roads. The one which runs by the sea is a fast dual carriageway. The second road, C812, is of more interest as it goes inland enabling you to visit several busy Canarian towns.

At **Carrizal** the Artesania La Molina (the windmill), a school of needlework, is open to visitors. Girls are seen at work on the *calados,* which is a fine embroidery of drawn thread work, used for mats, tablecloths and clothes. From an early age, young girls are taught very intricate sewing. Much embroidery work is done in Canarian country homes during the summer months, when women have finished working in the fields on the tomato crops that grow from October to April.

Ingenio used to be an old colonial town with sugar cane crops, (*ingenio* means sugar plantation). Now it, too, has a school of needlework open to the public. At the edge of the town is a modern distillery where gin and liqueurs are bottled. Nearby is the Barranco Guayadeque, noted for its Guanche caves and quiet scenery, a

*Pine wood is still used to make these old style balconies which adorn
so many Canarian houses.*

popular place for walking and well worth a visit.

Three kilometres further south is the important town of **Agüimes,** once the seat of the Bishops of the Canaries between the fifteenth and nineteenth century. The bell towers and domes of the mighty Church of San Sebastián dominate the landscape. The older part of the town has very narrow streets that are not recommended for driving. There is a useful petrol station on the southern outskirts of Agüimes, where the road divides to go inland to Temisas or south to Arinaga. While at Agüimes you might like to make a short detour further inland on the C815 to visit **Lomo de Los Letreros** in the ravine of Balos.

Back on the coast again, there is **Arinaga,** a small port used to export local produce; close by is a light industry estate. **Vecindario** and **El Doctoral** are well populated Canarian towns, not catering for the tourists, so the shops provide commodities usually at lower prices than in the coastal resorts. These would be useful places to find a motor engineer or to have a repair job done.

The C812 joins the coastal road again by the sea at the **Aero Club de Canaria** but just before you reach the Aero Club there is a Go-Kart track, open from 1000 to 2300 hrs, with Karts for all ages. It also has two bars, a restaurant and games room, and seats for spectators. Now the road approaches the great tourist area of the south and, as if by magic, gone are the dusty bare expanses, all hidden by apartments and villas. *Urbanizacións,* as these complexes are called, have sprung up like mushrooms in the past ten years.

As the road winds near the coast, on both sides of the road civilisation has taken over in a big way. Some of the *urbanizacións* have been designed in an artistic manner and have names like 'Canary Village' and 'Sun Valley', others have fallen foul of the economic times and have not been completed. Bahia Feliz has hotel apartment blocks, shops, pool and attractive gardens. It is a quiet place for a vacation, yet within reach of the holiday spots and amusements.

It is at **San Agustin,** 25 kilometres south of the airport, with its sandy beach, that the whole area starts to be fully developed.

A wonderful place to get a sun tan, the beach at Playa del Inglés has seven kilometres of soft sands.

TEN

The south-east

Island tour 2

San Agustin — Playa del Inglés — Palmitos Park — Playa de Maspalomas: about 30km

At the quieter end of the tourist coast, San Agustin has a casino which is part of the Hotel Tamarindos, with its own entrance from the road at Playa San Agustin. The casino is open from 2000 to 0300 hrs except Saturdays when the hours are from 2100 to 0400; closed Sunday evening. A passport is necessary to gain admission and gentlemen are expected to wear a jacket and tie. Games include French and American roulette, blackjack, chemin de fer and punto y banca. Gambling is strictly controlled by a government representative on duty throughout the evening. With its high class hotels, situated close to the sea, San Agustin caters for selective tourists.

A shopping centre at San Agustin, built on three floors, includes restaurants, bars, cafés, supermarkets, tourist shops, ironmongers, newsagents, boutiques, hairdressing salon and public toilets.

Down on the seafront it is possible to walk for several kilometres along a promenade that borders streets of villas and bungalows, many with colourful gardens. This part of the coast is favoured by wind surfing enthusiasts, the bright sails and graceful movement on the blue sea giving vivid splashes of colour.

Playa del Inglés
From San Agustin the main highway runs into **Playa del Inglés/Maspalomas,** the main tourist area of Gran Canaria. This is the boom town of the Canaries. Twenty years ago it was an isolated fishing village with a lighthouse on the edge of the sand dunes. Gradually Europeans, especially Germans and Scandinavians,

realised how magnificent the climate remained all year round. So it started with villas and bungalows, then hotels and apartment blocks were built, and more and more land was developed. Now it is a vast vacation land, its six kilometres of golden sands, warm sea waters and constant sunshine providing a holiday paradise. Endless cafés, bars and restaurants cater for every nationality and taste. Dancing, discos, night clubs, dog racing, bingo and sports of every kind can be enjoyed at Playa del Inglés and Maspalomas; even a camel ride!

A comfortable way of exploring part of Playa del Inglés is to take the 'Mini Train' from outside the Supermarket El Veril in Avenida Italia, which leaves every half hour from 1000 to 1200 hrs and 1600 to 2200 hrs. This little train runs along the main streets and has open carriages, the journey takes 50 minutes. Another method of getting about for those who do not have a driving licence and do not wish to walk, is to hire a bicycle or moped.

Supermarkets, travel agents and rent-a-car firms abound in Playa del Inglés, many are attached to hotels. Shopping centres (called *commercials*) are grouped conveniently. One built like an Arab *souk* is called El Kasbah and has many African and Indian traders who will enjoy bartering for your custom.

For many the greatest attraction of all is the wonderful beach. Every morning it is a fascinating sight to see hordes of tourists of all shapes, sizes and nationalities emerge from hundreds of apartments, villas and hotels all making for the beach. No wonder, for the sands are soft and clean and the sea is mostly calm and safe for swimming. Layout chairs with sunshades are for hire, beach cafés can provide full meals and drinks. A large car park is right by the sea. Each day vast numbers walk the sands, in the morning going westwards towards the sand dunes; at midday the stream returns, only to be repeated in the afternoon, an almost continuous procession of bodies all aiming to get as tanned as possible. The very hardy walkers will stride out as far as **Playa de Maspalomas,** eight kilometres away, have their lunch at a beach bar, then return to Playa del Inglés in the afternoon. Quite an energetic way to spend a day even if one does have dips in the sea to cool down.

Nowadays the Spanish authorities acquiesce to the demand for naturist sunbathing. At Playa del Inglés the western end of the beach has notice boards proclaiming that nudism is permitted. This mainly takes place amongst the sand dunes.

Take care that you do not get sunburnt here. Another point regarding health is drinking water. Because of the water shortage, especially in Playa del Inglés, the addition of chemicals for purification tends to give drinking water a strong and unpleasant taste. It is wiser to drink bottled water, such as *Firgas* which is available in supermarkets, aerated or still.

Playa del Inglés abounds with restaurants, cafés and bars dispensing food suitable for all nationalities. Service is good. The majority of establishments have live or taped music and a wide range of night life to suit all ages and tastes is at hand.

In recent years mass tourist development has allowed bungalows to be built along both sides of the road, leading from Playa del Inglés to Playa de Maspalomas. The result is an unsightly sprawl, a real nightmare of concrete and a horrific example of lack of care for the environment. The beautiful natural sand dunes of Maspalomas have been smothered. Almost too late the remaining dunes have now been declared an area of natural beauty and are to be preserved. Unfortunately the lagoon, once a place favoured by migratory birds, has been turned into a fishing and boating lake. Nearby is the Maspalomas Golf Club, an oasis of greens and trees. Along the road is Ocean Park, a popular water park with all the usual amenities. Close by is Holiday World, a huge noisy fun fair with big wheels, roller coasters and amusement stalls; a cheery place for children with plenty of holiday spending money.

Palmitos Park

Another attraction is **Palmitos Park** (see Chapter 4, Excursions). There is a free bus service between here and Playa del Inglés. A taxi from here or Maspalomas could cost you 1000 pesetas (£5.15), and from San Agustin 1220 pesetas (£6.28). To reach Palmitos Park by car you must turn right off the main road after leaving Playa del Inglés, (signposted Parrot Park) and drive up the **Barranco de Chamoriscan** to the Parrot Park. On the way a left-hand turn leads to El Tablero where there are some pensions, restaurants and sometimes Canary Wrestling *(lucha Canaria)* to be seen.

It is a pleasant drive up the *barranco* past a German riding school, a Go-kart track (open from 1000 hrs until midnight) and a newly erected **Water Park.** There is also a restaurant here, El Alamo. A turning off this road to the right leads to Monte Leon, a millionaire's hide out, where magnificent villas are perched on mountain peaks. The bird sanctuary is located almost at the top of the *barranco,* amid lush greenery, colourful flora and tall palm trees. Past the aviary is the tennis hotel, Helga Mastof. If you like walking you can continue on foot on a dusty track that overlooks the pretty Ayagaures Valley and continue to the tiny hamlet of Ayagaures Alto, by the Embalse de Ayagaures and the dam of Gambueda. Stout footwear is required.

Footsteps in the sand: these marvellous Sahara-like dunes provide a natural location for your overall sun tan.

Playa de Maspalomas

Returning down the barranco from Palmitos Park to the main road, the C182, where there are traffic lights, take the road south leading to the sea and signed **Faro de Maspalomas** (lighthouse). You will see the tall tower as you speed towards the large car park in front of it. Here buses, coaches, taxis and cars every day disgorge their passengers, all armed with sun hats, sun glasses, buckets and spades, heading for what they have come for, sea and sunshine. Most days they will be satisfied. On the beach are sunbeds and sun and wind shields, for both can be fierce at times. Several luxury hotels are secluded behind high fences and exotic gardens, filled with tall palm trees. A long walkway *(paseo)* from the bus stops is lined with cafés, restaurants, souvenir shops, knick-knack stalls and a useful newsagent where, if you wish, you can buy a British newspaper or paperback novel.

Behind the flat white beach, the Sahara like sand dunes make excellent hideaway shelters for that overall tan. But once again we do warn of the real danger of over exposure to the sun and wind, even with the use of sun tan lotions. Sunstroke can be most unpleasant, even dangerous, and remember also that the wind, too, can burn the skin. Another note of caution: do not leave anything in the interior of your car, and as little as possible locked in the boot. Travel light and you will be safer, especially at well known tourist spots.

By the lighthouse, what was once a track going west along the coast, amid green tomato fields, will now be made into a road leading to Meloneras Playa. The tomato fields are now fast disappearing.

The Campo de Golf, amongst the Maspalomas sand dunes, is a veritable green oasis providing pleasant golf by the sea.

ELEVEN

The south

Island tour 3

Playa de Maspalomas — Playa Meloneras — Pasito Blanco — Cercado de Espino — Soria — Arguineguin — Patalavaca — Puerto Rico: about 18 km

At the road junction, where the main road C182 turns westwards from Maspalomas, a Texaco petrol filling station provides a 24-hour service but is closed on Sundays. Following the main coastal route westwards the countryside remains bare and arid, and the central mountains are still to be seen inland. Despite the poor soil, it is in this part of Gran Canaria that huge crops of outdoor tomatoes are grown, the bamboo canes supporting them standing in near-perfect straight rows. In the past tomatoes have made an important contribution to the economy and, despite the great tourist invasion, they are still grown in vast quantities. Conditions for a lot of workers are still primitive, many living in what are virtually shacks in 'shanty towns', the children running barefoot, and whole families work in the fields. Irrigation is by a series of water channels that are strictly controlled, often by just a dam of mud. The precious water is piped from the high mountains and retained in reservoirs. During the winter months, the Canarians look longingly for rain whenever a few clouds gather, while tourists invariably hope for sunshine! An interesting fact is that because the tomato crop is picked for export when green, it is not always easy to buy ripe tomatoes in the shops.

Meloneras and Pasito Blanco

Amongst the tomato fields and about 2 kms west of the Texaco petrol station, a turning seawards down a rough unmade road leads to **Meloneras Playa.** A privately-owned beach open to the public, it has a small seaside bar that serves lunches at tables on the sands.

Most of the year the beach has plenty of sand and provides splendid swimming, and it is popular with wind surfers. During the winter months when gales out in the Atlantic can send in huge waves, it has happened that the sand has been washed away leaving only rocks and pebbles; luckily the sand returns. This beach is a favourite haunt for motorcaravanners who, during the winter months, love to find a peaceful venue close to the sea. Now planning permission has been given to develop Meloneras as a beach resort. No longer will visiting motorcaravanners, together with their Canarian camping friends, forgather for a beach barbecue and a night by the seashore. Happy memories!

A further kilometre or so west at **Pasito Blanco** is a newly-built marine harbour, the **Puerto de Club de Yates,** a yacht club with modern facilities including apartments, ships' chandler and post office.

Almost opposite to the yacht marina is the entrance to Pasito Blanco Camping Park (see Chapter 3, Camping).

The main highway continues to wind its way very close to the sea, and some of the bends require careful attention. Approaching **Arguineguin,** there is a large cement factory built on a jetty; the bay is always busy with shipping. In the same area, behind concrete walls, a banana plantation stretches either side of the road.

Cercado de Espino and Soria

Here a turning to the right is signposted to **Cercado de Espino,** and a pleasant detour or evening drive can be made up this dry Barranco de Arguineguin. Allow time, for the road is broken in places, but it becomes a scenic route higher up the valley as you progress. On either side the brown, craggy mountains are clothed in green almost to the top ridges. Down on the floor of the valley the sweet perfume of orange groves, avocado and vines meets you as you pass by El Sao. In March, wild flowers bloom along the roadside. Here the yellow sonchus, purple senecio, feathery pink tamarisk and the white echiums are but a few of the more easily recognised species.

As you approach Cercado de Espino tall palm trees add to the peaceful scene. A long narrow, winding street leads up to this quiet mountain village, where the only busy place is Castillo Ramon. Open all the year, this German run restaurant has an attractive decor and if you can time your visit to miss the coach parties you can then enjoy some tranquil refreshment. If you make your visit on a Friday or Sunday evening, there is live music and dancing; at times donkey rides, too.

Should you have a vehicle with a four-wheel drive, then we

suggest that you press on further up this beautiful valley and make for the **Presa de Soria.** This is a really adventurous drive and not for anyone likely to suffer with vertigo, as the narrow road has few passing places and its steep edges could have you clutching the door handle. It is a wonderful, isolated place that few tourists reach. By a simple bar restaurant in Soria a track leads to the dam wall, where if you wish you can enjoy a unique picnic away from the crowds.

On your return down the barranco you will be surprised that your views seem totally different as you face the sunshine. Watch for chickens scratching in the dust as you pass isolated homesteads.

Arguineguin to Puerto Rico

Arguineguin, once a sleepy fishing village, is now developing into an important fishing port. Several good supermarkets, a petrol station, a camping Gaz stockist, post office and restaurants have encouraged tourists to aid and expand the growth. Yet, today, it has managed to retain its original Canarian character. The Tuesday open air market is a meeting place for locals and holiday makers who mingle cheerfully.

Recently a useful seashore walk has been constructed between Arguineguin and **Patalavaca,** so avoiding the busy winding cliff road. In past times, before the coast road was built, the women workers carried heavy baskets of tomatoes on their heads, down from mountain villages to the jetty at Patalavaca to be shipped to Las Palmas. This arduous work was a great strain on them and it is said their life expectancy rarely reached forty. Thankfully those days of toil are fast disappearing, although around Arguineguin one still sees some pathetic shanty communities and bare foot children, but they look healthy.

The winding coastal road continues on past modern *urbanizatións* of apartments, some luxurious and attractive, their balconies ablaze with geraniums and bougainvillea. All have their own swimming pools and supermarkets. There is also a five-star hotel, La Canaria.

Going through a short tunnel the road reaches **Puerto Rico,** a man-made oasis built entirely for the tourist. Sand was brought from the Sahara Desert to make a beach. This sheltered bay has perhaps the most favourable climate in all Gran Canaria and its theme is luxury, leisure and sport. Indeed, during January and February, the coolest months, coach loads of tourists are brought daily from Las Palmas, where it can be cloudy and cool, to enjoy Puerto Rico's sunshine. Consequently the tiny beach becomes packed with bodies, but it has a happy carefree atmosphere.

On either side of the hills that surround Puerto Rico, hundreds of apartments are set in long terraces, with roads running down to the beach below. In the centre of Puerto Rico are parks that are a sheer joy — a profusion of ornamental trees and tropical shrubs. Green grass grows as if by magic in the dry soil and paths wind under exotic trees, as if in a fairytale garden. Carparks, swimming pools, tennis courts and restaurants have been planned into this colourful plantation.

A *centro commercial* (shopping precinct) has open-fronted shops selling a varied range of tourist requirements and souvenirs. Leather and brasswork from Africa; transistors, watches and cameras from Japan; ceramics and textiles from Spain; jewellery, silver, gold and porcelain all mingle with cheap toys and ornaments to lure the peseta from your pocket.

Nearer the beach by the busy roads that criss-cross in the centre of Puerto Rico, are the banks, post office and telephones. An underpass tunnel is helpful when the roads are busy. Supermarkets, self-drive car rentals, travel agents, newsagents and many boutiques can be found here.

Two roads lead to two separate harbours, both used by yachts and private pleasure boats. At **Puerto Nuevo** the new port, two old red-sailed sailing ships, the 'Gefion' and the 'San Miguel' make

Deep sea game fishing is a most exciting sport. Powerful boats sail out of Puerto Rico daily in search of marlin, shark, tunny and other big fish.

Holidaymakers exercise daily, walking between Playa del Inglés and Playa de Maspalomas, where there are bars close to the sea.

daily tourist excursions out to sea, except Mondays. The full-day trip includes a meal with wine and entertainment, an opportunity to swim and assist with sailing the ship. A day at sea is also offered in the motor vessels 'Hai Turn' and 'Alexandria', when shark fishing can be part of the day's fun. Shorter trips can be made on the 'Sea Safari', which offers a two-hour trip along the coast. During this excursion fresh fish is barbecued and wine drunk; the crew say anyone can go with them — except pirates!

The latest attraction at Puerto Rico is a yellow plastic submarine, not a toy but one that takes forty-eight passengers below the surface of the sea, to observe the marine life and the many fish that swim along the coast. Inland, by the shopping centre, is yet another Water Park.

Puerto Rico has acquired fame all over the world as a big game fishing centre. For centuries fishermen have been chasing tuna, bonita, shark, barracuda and swordfish. Nowadays amateur sports fishermen as well as professionals participate, and nothing is more exciting than to be on the quay at Puerto Rico between 1530 and 1630 hrs, when the powerful little fishing boats return, and everyone is eager to see the day's catch being sorted, weighed and often photographed. Fishermen exchange stories, tourists gaze in amazement and waiters start laying tables in the restaurants. Puerto

Rico has many restaurants that specialise in international cooking, but the fresh fish is the best. There are no night clubs in Puerto Rico but several restaurants have music and dancing and some of the apartments have discos.

Successful wind surfing, water ski and sailing schools operate in the harbour, the calm waters being ideal for beginners.

Unfortunately the developers have surely over-built at Puerto Rico; even the top of the dry, brown mountain behind this lovely horseshoe bay is now full of villas and apartments, and still the bulldozers crash their way into the rocky soil, creating more rabbit-hutch accommodation and man-made beaches. Yet, despite this eyesore of concrete, down by the harbours the atmosphere is relaxed and happy, with holidaymakers gently paddling a pedalo, or suntanning on the beach. Others enjoy an icecream or beer as they wait for the shark fishing boats to return. Then out come the cameras to record the catches, be they tiny mackerel or huge tunny. The holiday atmosphere is abundant at Puerto Rico.

(Opposite) *An unusual sight at Puerto Rico is this yellow submarine, waiting to take visitors to explore the colourful marine life.* (overleaf) *In front of the sand dunes at Playa de Maspalomas* (above) *stretch flat golden sands. Amazing mixtures of coloured rock strata* (below) *can be seen on the road side between Mogán and San Nicolas. In the foreground are brilliant poinsettias.*

TWELVE

The west

Island tour 4

Puerto Rico — Tauro — Puerto de Mogan — Mogan — Veneguera — San Nicolás de Tolentino — Puerto de la Aldea — Puerto de las Nieves: about 95kms

Still travelling along the coast, westwards from Puerto Rico at a very sharp bend you will pass a series of newly built chalets and bungalows, with manmade beaches below.

Near Tauro, in the *barrancos* there are small *urbanizacións* of bungalows and villas which are occupied — some all the year round though the majority only during the winter months — by foreigners, who enjoy a warm climate. The valleys also contain Canarian homesteads where chickens, tomatoes and avocado trees give life to the dry landscape. Fields of bananas and aubergines help to provide an income for those Canarians who still resist the temptation of the tourist trade and prefer to work the land.

Set in the centre of Playa de Tauro are the permanent campsites of Guantanamo, with supermarket and restaurant on the sea side of the road (see Chapter 3, Camping). The pebble and sand beach of Tauro gives pleasant swimming when the seas are calm, but at high tide it may have a strong undercurrent.

The C812 road continues to hug the coastline in great sweeping bends and when the traffic is not heavy it is a lovely drive by the blue Atlantic. Inland the dry dusty volcanic mountains are full of caves and crevices with weird shaped rock formations. If you see white lines painted on the rock face, you will know they are doomed for development. Just before reaching Puerto de Mogan you will pass Taurito Tropical, once a favourite beach for nudists. Now it has become a modern complex, said to contain six thousand beds; it appears to be one of the better developed bays with an impressive blue and white archway entrance, tropical gardens, swimming pool and bar restaurant.

Around the next bend in the road you see the beginning of the **Barranco de Mogan,** a green fertile valley. The road sweeps down to a T-junction and a petrol station. The right hand branch goes to the village of Mogan, while the left leads to the sea at Puerto de Mogan; a prize development in Gran Canaria and well worth visiting.

Until recent years **Puerto de Mogan** could only be reached by sea, and the extension of the coastal road has considerably altered the village. Nowadays TV aerial masts are seen at the top of the high cliffs reaching down to the cluster of houses below. The harbour, recently modernised and enlarged, now has some attractive apartments built over the water. Joined by small arched bridges it is reminiscent of Venice. Fish restaurants and moored yachts add to the picturesque scene. A small beach has been covered with sand; layout chairs and sun umbrellas are available.

Returning to the main road and going inland the way becomes narrower as it climbs through the *barranco* between fields of crops for nine kilometres to the village of **Mogan.** Set on the mountainside, this typically Canarian *pueblo* has only a sprinkling of foreign residents. A few tourist shops and bars are easily located. Being well above sea level, Mogan is favoured by a little rainfall each year and a moist climate, hence the cultivation. In the gardens oranges, lemons, grapefruit, papaya and coffee grow well. Tall palms and vivid shrubs like bougainvillea, poinsettia and geraniums all make it an attractive place. Unfortunately progress is catching up with this quiet village; now it has one-way streets and several unsightly modern buildings.

Leaving Mogan the road improves; a newly constructed two-lane highway winds on up into the mountains, giving panoramic views of much beauty. Strata of volcanic rock create spectacular shapes and sizes, quite awesome, overpowering even. The completion of this piece of roadwork has made it possible to drive in a complete circle round the island.

At the head of the barranco at Puerto de Cuesta, lies an attractive rustic restaurant, El Arauillo. A side track here is the route through the mountains to Tejeda, only to be undertaken with a suitable vehicle. Continuing uphill to San Nichol one sees nestling down below the road the Moorish village of **Veneguera,** in a pretty setting with palm trees and tropical plants.

Seawards past this village the tarmac runs out at present, only a rough ride reaches down to the playa. No doubt the developers will soon arrive here, too.

Still twisting and turning our road now passes some amazing rock colourings, shading from pale yellow, dusty pink to deep red and brilliant hues of blue and green. You are sure to make a stop for an unusual photograph. Nearby an enterprising Canarian has set up a small café for refreshments.

Another stopping place is where the mountain opens up so that from the viewpoint *(mirador)* you can look back towards Mogan and to the north over the great expanse that leads to San Nicolás de Tolentino. A side road here branches off seawards to the isolated hamlet of Tasartico. In Noel Rochford's book *Landscapes of Gran Canaria* (see Bibliography) he gives a very explicit description of a walk to Playa de Güigüi, which ends at Tasartico. This remote beach can only be reached from the sea or on foot at present. Five kilometres before San Nicolás de Tolentino is a layby which gives fabulous view over the massive valley, high mountains and the port way below. On clear days you can see the coastline of Tenerife.

San Nicolás de Tolentino is an important municipality on the west coast. Because of its sheltered position it has always been an area of intense cultivation. Bananas, tomatoes, cucumbers, some sugar cane and, more recently, the growth of splendid carnations gives plenty of work for the people of the region. Here you will see women wearing straw hats, and laughing pretty girls working in the fields and in the plastic covered greenhouses. Old men in black felt hats sit on the side of the road and will return your smile with a dignified nod of the head.

The town sprawls out in an unplanned manner, a few pensions and some new bars and restaurants cater for the passing tourist. No longer cheap, the menus tend to be international. That often means chicken and chips, but do try the local Canarian soup, it is usually a meal in itself. Of recent years water and bread are charged on the bill. With the coming of cars, fridges and television the country folk are learning fast about modern practices.

While here make the short drive to **Puerto de la Aldea.** The port has a new promenade and a peaceful atmosphere. It is said that around here the fossilised bones of the *verdino,* the ancient Canary dogs, were discovered. In September this is the venue for the important Fiesta del Charco, when palm leaves are thrown into the sea to ensure good weather and prosperity for the coming year.

The C810 road now climbs very steeply, twisting and winding its way northwards to Puerto de las Nieves, 44 km away. Often the sea is turquoise blue with good views over the Atlantic. On clear days the peak of Mount Teide on Tenerife is seen, snow capped and amazingly beautiful, a perfect cone of white in the blue sky. Time is needed to drive along this stretch of road, for the countryside is wild, with little habitation, and many twists and bends have unguarded edges that drop sharply away to the sea.

Although only forty-four kilometres from Aldea this drive can be quite tiring, with endless twists and sharp corners. It is sensible to sound your horn as you approach narrow bends, because buses, coaches and huge trucks use this route to reach Las Palmas. You are likely to sigh with relief when you see ahead of you the compact little port of **Puerto de Las Nieves** and after your exhilarating coastal drive you will be glad to have some refreshment and stretch your legs.

Puerto de las Nieves, (Port of the Snows) is said to have been given its name because of the views of Mount Teide. Swimming is possible on the two small shingle beaches, which are sheltered under a high headland of basalt cliffs. A curious rock formation is called **El Dedo de Dios** (Finger of God) because it points towards heaven. Several restaurants 'tipico' are to be found along the narrow streets by the seafront; no longer simple fish bars, they now cater for a constant flow of visitors, with corresponding prices. As elsewhere, this port is being developed and the plans include yacht moorings and marina facilities.

THIRTEEN

The north

Island tour 5

**Puerto de las Nieves — Agaete — Los Berrazales —
Sardina — Galdar — Guia — Las Palmas: about 63 km**

A distance of 2 kms northwards from Puerto de las Nieves brings
the road to **Agaete,** a quiet peaceful town. Its hermitage, Ermita de
la Nieves, has one of the islands great treasures, a beautiful
sixteenth-century triptych showing La Virgen de la Nieves, the
Virgin of the Snows. Every August a fiesta is held which is a mixture
of religious ceremonies and processions and folk dancing. In the
main streets tourist shops have a wide range of souvenirs, and
several houses with typical Canarian wooden balconies are to be
seen. At the very end of the road is a hotel where visitors may use
the restaurant. It is a little 'paradise' place, tucked away from the
modern world.

The Agaete Valley of **Los Berrazales** is one of the most fertile in
Gran Canaria, just 7 kms in length; the moist air from the
surrounding mountains creates a green 'Garden of Eden' which is
a pleasure to behold, especially if one has been staying in the
sunbaked, arid south. Grass grows amongst wild geraniums,
marigolds and dog-roses along the verges. The aroma of pine trees,
jasmine and honeysuckle sweetens the air and tall palm trees stand
out picturesquely against the reddish cultivated soil.

At the end of the narrow valley ferruginous water tumbles down
from the mountainside. Once there was the Banos de Agaete, a
hotel where rheumatic sufferers could bathe in the waters, but sadly
its doors are now closed. However mineral water is still bottled at
a small factory and delivered all over the island. At the very end of
the road is a hotel where visitors may use the restaurant. It is a little
'paradise' place tucked away from the modern world.

Well worth a visit are the **Cuevas de las Cruces,** 5 kms north of
Agaete. These caves have been inhabited since ancient times and

remain cool in summer and warm in winter. The ownership of a cave is closely guarded by the family who pass it on to the next generation.

Beyond the caves you will see a minute little chapel, Ermita de San Isidro el Viejo, and a minor road leading up to Hoya de Pineda. This winding route is slow and rough in places, taking you through peaceful mountain scenery as it winds up and down slopes. There are various turn-offs, both north and south. Allow plenty of time if you wish to explore away from the beaten track.

The road from Agaete north is fast and soon you will see (past the caves) the volcanic cone of Montana Almagro.

At a junction 5 kms north of the caves, the road turns westwards to the coast and **Sardina,** set amid acres of banana plantations. Sardina houses a small community of Canarians who mostly work on the plantations or make a living by fishing from the tiny port. A small hotel on the seafront is closed during the winter but the restaurant may be open, serving fresh fish.

A turning off the road to Sardina leads to a new visitors' centre, Reptilandia Park. A large sign is by the main Agaete-Galdar road. A winding lane leads along the slopes of Montana Almagro to a panoramic site where this specialist zoo is situated. Here an enterprising Englishman and his Spanish partner have created a unique set-up, which is for research work as well as a business venture. Lots of creeping crawling creatures and endearing marmosets are included in this fascinating collection of over a hundred reptiles (see Chapter 4, Excursions).

The next town is **Galdar** on the north coast which, with neighbouring **Guia,** is of some historical importance. Galdar was the capital of the Guanche kingdom and some Guanche relics are preserved in the town hall, which is opposite the church in the Plaza Mayor (main square), which also houses an ancient dragon tree. Both these towns are agricultural centres, set amid vineyards and banana plantations, and heavily populated with Canarians. Worth a visit if you can find a carpark. The *queso* (cheese) of the area is famous: *queso de flor* (flower cheese) is made from goats milk and thistle flowers. It is a great favourite in the Canaries and Spain and is exported to many countries in Europe. It can be purchased in Harrods, the London store.

It is just a few kilometres on the coast road from Guia to the **Cenobio de Valeron,** a notable archaeological site where hundreds of caves are to be seen in the cliff face. The place has an eerie atmosphere. It is thought to have been a convent where Guanche maidens worshipped a divinity called Alcorac. During the Spanish

Cooking Canarian

The frugal and natural diet of the Canarians has been handed down from one generation to the next. A traditional food is *gofio,* a kind of gruel made by using toasted cereals, such as maize, wheat, barley or even chick peas. With the addition of milk, salt, honey and dried fruits *golfio* becomes a favourite breakfast dish, similar to Scottish porridge. Sometimes the *gofio* is rolled into small balls and put into a cloth, then boiled to be served with a stew of meat or fish.

Another old recipe is *mojo,* a piquant sauce. *Mojo Palmero* is a red hot sauce made from red peppers, garlic, sweet peppers, cumin, oil and vinegar. *Mojo* is served with little wrinkled potatoes *(papas arrugadas)* cooked in their skins in a little salt water, which are a true Canarian staple food. Sometimes the *mojo* has crushed almonds or grated bread added. In Gomera they make a delicious mojo with grated cheese, known as *almogrote gomera.* Another variant is to substitute fresh green coriander leaves for the hot pepper to make *mojo de Cilantro* or *mojo verde,* which is served with fish dishes. Add a little natural yoghurt to the *mojo* sauce, which makes it really creamy.

invasion the caves became a Guanche refuge and look-out post over the surrounding countryside.

Just beyond Guia the main road becomes a two-lane highway which keeps close to the coast. It gives good views of the Atlantic and the cultivated areas of the north of Gran Canaria, with dark *barrancos* making deep indentations into the central mountains. Modern viaducts and tunnels have made this route fast. A turning inland, the C813, leads to Arucas (nearby is a Texaco petrol station open twenty four hours). The rest of the journey is rather dull with its rocky shoreline. Past Banadero you reach the outer city limits, and a winding route through the back streets of Las Palmas. So the circular tour of Gran Canaria is complete.

The splendid Church of Nuestra Señora del Pino, in the centre of Teror, is a popular stopping place for coach tours. Nearby is a Canarian mansion open to the public.

FOURTEEN

Touring inland

Inland route 1

Moya — Firgas — Balcon de Zamora — Teror — Arucas — Las Palmas; about 77 km

An alternative route from Guia to Las Palmas can be enjoyed by taking the road to **Moya,** which affords a scenic drive into the green north of Gran Canaria, where fields of corn and grazing cattle mingle with vines and potato crops. Heavy oxen till the soil, the small farmhouses are pretty with white wash and flowers. Carnations grow well here and are produced commercially.

Moya is a spread-out town perched on the edge of a steep *barranco,* the huge twin towers of its church making a striking picture from a distance. The s ronghold of the last Guanche King Doramas, it is also the birthplace of Tomas Morales, the Canarian poet (1885 to 1921).

The road continues to twist and turn up and down *barrancos* sometimes in a pine forest, then by a river bed. A fork left leads to **Firgas,** famous for its spring waters, which are bottled and sold throughout the Canary Islands. The mineral water is sold *con gas* (aerated) and *sin gas* (still). The bottling plant is out of the village on the road to Vallesco. At the **Balcon de Zamora** on the Vallesco road a view-point allows an extensive vista of the fertile green valley below. A large restaurant, much used by coach tours, serves freshly cooked meals. *Tapas* (snacks) can be had at the bar.

The same road now climbs higher and higher through a series of pine forests to the centre of the island and Cruz de Tejeda. But our route takes us just six kilometres down a zig zag road to the important town of **Teror** set in a peaceful valley. The major point of interest is the large Canarian church of Nuestra Señora del Pino. This splendid shrine draws great numbers of the faithful, especially on 8 September when the Fiesta de la Virgen del Pino takes place. She takes her name from the pine tree that fell when the Virgin Mary is said to have made an appearance to the priest of the village. The beautiful alabaster image is enthroned in the church, which dates from 1767. Richly dressed in heavily embroidered robes, the image is set on high, surrounded by cherubs, holding incense bowls. The wonderful silver canopy is said to be the work of a celebrated eighteenth-century silversmith from Tenerife.

Teror is a delightful Canarian town with carved pine balconies along its quiet streets. In the large square outside the church are several small tourist shops. Some of the embroidered needlework and lace is made by the nuns at the local convent. If you are looking for an heirloom the work is exquisite.

Just across the square from the church is the House of the Patrons of Our Lady of the Pines, an old Canarian mansion open to the public. The house has belonged to the family of Manrique de la Lara (a noble surname) since the seventeenth century and is still used by the family for summer holidays. It contains valuable silver and glassware, furniture and ornaments.

From Teror it is fifteen kilometres north via El Palmar to **Arucas** which is the third largest town, eighteen kilometres from Las Palmas, set in a fertile plain with important banana plantations stretching in all directions. Montana de Arucas, an old volcanic cone, affords fine views of the town and the north coast as far as Las Palmas. An outstanding feature of Arucas is the parish church, St Juan Bautista, more like a cathedral. Although built as recently as 1909, the Gothic style gives it a much older appearance. Many fine old colonial houses are to be seen in Arucas which has busy streets and a large municipal car park.

To get the feel of the island go into one of the small bars in the town and have a coffee or something stronger. Order a doughnut filled with custard cream, or something savoury such as *tortilla* (Spanish omelette) or *papas arrugadas,* the tiny Canarian potatoes eaten with the local piquant sauce *mojo,* which is made from peppers, oil, vinegar and spices. It is perfectly acceptable for unaccompanied females to use the bars. Often one sees quite young children with their mothers, enjoying a Coke and crisps.

Excursion parties visiting Arucas are taken around a banana plantation, with a guide to explain the development of the plant in all stages of its growth. Visitors are able to purchase bananas fresh from the trees. Arucas is also the centre of the rum industry. This spirit, made from the locally grown cane, is very popular with Canarians.

Carnival

The word carnival derives from the Latin meaning 'the cessation of meat', and traditionally carnival takes place in February or March, with people allowing themselves a final celebration before beginning the fasting and self-denial of the Lenten period.

All the Canary Islands celebrate at least one week of Carnival. This 'winter festival' is looked on by all Canarians as the happiest time of the year, when for a few days they put aside their worries and problems to dress up in something bright and cheerful and go out into the streets to sing and dance the nights away. There are often fireworks to help the party along.

Local bands have been rehearsing their pieces and dance groups practising their steps for months. In homes all over the islands people have been stitching coloured fabrics, often star-spangled or glittering gold and silver, into elaborate costumes; thousands of sequins, pearls, feathers and lace go to make the carnival costumes with wigs and masks to add to the fun. Even private cars are sometimes given some 'fancy dress'. The election of Carnival Queen and Junior Queen is taken seriously.

The day of the grand carnival procession (the *coso*) starts at dawn, with road sweepers singing their way along the streets. Shops are closed, restaurants and bars prepare for a busy time (though Canarian fiestas are not a time for drunken rowdyism).

All day people arrive from towns and villages to forgather in chattering family groups. Never on time, the start of the parade is accompanied by many noisy bands cheerfully blasting away. Then the groups follow, each being cheered and clapped with enthusiasm.

The arrival of the Queen brings gasps of pleasure. She and her attendant maids sit atop a large float on a golden throne, her ornate high headdress of feathers waving in the breeze as she acknowledges the cheers of the crowd. Clowns, Micky Mouse, King Kong, lions, tigers, witches, tramps — all these and many more pass in a kaleidoscope of colour. At the heart of the carnival are the spectacularly dressed groups (the *comparas*) that rumba, samba and salsa their way, Rio-style, down the streets.

And when it is all over, the groups — often one family from grandmother down to the baby in a pushchair, and all dressed alike — will wander to the funfair to enjoy deep fried doughnuts *(churros),* toffee apples *(manzana garrapunda),* steak filled rolls *(pepitos)* and, best of all, spicy pork kebabs *(pinchitos),* and drink rum and cola *(una cubata).*

The journey from Arucas to Las Palmas on the C810 is only eighteen kilometres but because the road winds through several *barrancos* with many undulations and in some places is narrow,

In the centre of this panorama is the Gothic style church at Arucas, surrounded by large banana plantations.

allow yourself about an hour to reach the city. Driving through Tenoya and Tamaraceite you will see more fertile banana plantations, which continue to the outskirts of Las Palmas city.

Inland route 2

Las Palmas — Jardin Botanico Canario — Monte Cello — Caldera Bandama — Santa Brigida — San Mateo — Pozo de las Nieves — Cruz de Tejeda — Las Palmas: about 94 km return

From Las Palmas it is only thirty five kilometres to the centre of the island and its highest point, Pozo de las Nieves, 1392 m. From Las Palmas take the C811, a fast motorway, for about seven kilometres to **Tafira Baja,** which is really a continuation of Las Palmas city, and contains many expensive houses belonging to its prosperous businessmen.

Jardin Botanico Canario, the botanical gardens, are about eleven kilometres west of Las Palmas, along this road in the direction of Santa Brigida. There is free entrance into these important botanical gardens, situated in an area called Angostura. Open 1000 to 1200 and 1500 to 1800 hrs.

The beautiful Angostura Valley has an ideal climate for growing rare botanical species and the gardens contain a fine collection of native flora, including trees recently planted (1964) which have reached a great height. Represented here is the Canary laurel (Laurisilva), which has a slender trunk, light grey bark and dark green leathery leaves. These can be used as a spice, though they are not so flavoursome as the genuine laurel (sweet bay) leaves.

In the same area is **Monte Cello,** the island's best wine producing region — *vino tinto de Monte* is a pleasant and well-known local red wine.

From the C811 a detour is recommended to visit the **Caldera Bandama,** one of the wonders of Gran Canaria. This volcanic crater, some 609 m above sea level, has a peaceful green bowl 198 m deep and over a kilometre wide, with a flourishing farm at the bottom. Incidentally it is only possible to descend to the bottom on foot or by donkey. The Mirador de Bandama at the top of a high cone of land gives magnificent views in all directions, out to the mighty Atlantic and towards the centre and south of the island.

Nearby is the Club de Golf de las Palmas, 14 kms from Las Palmas, founded in 1891. It has an 18-hole course open all the year round, except Good Friday, and visitors are welcome. There is a bar-restaurant and horse-riding is available.

At **La Atalaya** are more Guanche caves, some quite close to the road, which are still in everyday use as homes and for storage. It is said that there are over one thousand caves here; a nearby centre for ceramics and basket work is useful for souvenir shopping.

Rejoining the C811 road it is a pleasant drive towards **Santa Brigida** through green hills and valleys, especially beautiful in February when the odd rain shower freshens the countryside and emphasises the sweet perfume of the almond blossom. The road winds its way in ever increasing height until it reaches **San Mateo** at 650 m. This village has a popular tourist attraction, the Casa de Cho Zacarias, an old farmhouse made into a rural museum. Typical rustic implements and Canary furniture are on show, and in a *bodega* visitors can sample the local cheese and wine. On Sundays a busy open air market attracts both tourists and Canarians; sales include live animals, especially goats.

Through an area of upland agriculture the road continues towards the mountain peaks. A turning off the main road leads almost to the top of the **Pozo de las Nieves,** 1950 m, affording wonderful views in a quiet and tranquil setting. In the distance can be seen the **Roque Nublo** (*nube* means cloud), a peak once held sacred by the Guanches and still awe-inspiring.

Cruz de Tejeda, accepted as the centre of the island, lies inland at a height of 1450 m. The Cross of Tejeda was a crucifix originally made of pine, which has now been replaced by a cross made of island stone. It stands in a square where tourist coaches park. Old men with bedecked donkeys tempt tourists to have a ride; beware, these genial old men will offer to use your camera to photograph you and your friends beside their donkey and expect payment! Small stalls, bars and a restaurant offer a wide selection of tourist gifts, a little more expensive than elsewhere, but for the tourist in a hurry it is a good place to buy things. The fruit and vegetables on sale are of the best quality; look for the really enormous avocado pears and local goat's cheese.

When standing near the Cruz de Tejeda you are unable to see any clear views because the area around is heavily forested. However a short walk down the road leads to gaps in the trees where, when the weather is clear, the views are extensive, looking over the high rock formations of the mountains of Gran Canaria and the distant snow peak of Mount Teide on Tenerife.

Inland route 3

Cruz de Tejeda — Artenara — Pinar de Tamadaba — Cruz de Tejeda: about 64 km

If you wish to explore further when at Cruz de Tejeda, a winding road north west, the GC 110, leads towards Artenara and Pinar de Tamadaba, providing a splendid drive with open views over mountains. After a short distance it enters an area of volcanic *malpais* (wasteland). Trees are now being planted here to join up with the natural forest of Tamadaba.

Artenara is the highest village on the island, at 1219 m, and it existed even before the Spanish invasion. Archaeological discoveries have been made here and it has its share of caves, the Cuevas de Acusa, once Guanche strongholds. Many cave dwellings are still occupied.

The **Meson de la Silla,** close to Artenara, is one of Gran Canaria's most delightful features. A hall carved out of rock leads to a restaurant located on a partially sheltered platform, from where there is a breathtaking view of the entire central mountain range. One should not forget to visit the chapel of Artenara's patron saint, the Virgen de Cuevita. The road to it is uphill almost opposite the church.

Pinar de Tamadaba is Gran Canaria's best known primeval forest, situated at an elevation of 1300 m and hidden in the central mountains. High and lonely, these wonderful forests consist almost entirely of *pinus Canariensis* (Canary pine) a tree found only in the Canaries. The trees, which often grow to a height of more than thirty metres, have pine needles that are exceptionally long.

The newly-made roads through the forest have a good surface and are of sufficient width to park a car at the side. There are few signposts, so it is sensible to have a road map with you. The Pico de Tamadaba, 1440 m, is a glorious summit that will appeal to lovers of nature, who will want to linger to enjoy the pure mountain air and peaceful isolation of the great forest.

Inland, the red-tiled houses of quiet villages nestle in the volcanic countryside, making a peaceful contrast to the coastal resorts.

Hikers and mountain climbers can continue on through the Barranco de Agaete to Los Berrazales and to the west coast. They will see countless rare plants in the crevices of the rocks and many wondrous views out across mountain peaks and uninhabited valleys below, before they finally reach sea level, near Agaete.

There is no easy road through the forest to the west coast so most tourists return by the same route, via Artenara to Cruz de Tejeda, thence to Las Palmas (but see also Inland route 5). Before completing the return trip a stop may be made at the Parador Nacional de Tejeda for refreshments in the restaurant; the entrance is close to the Cruz de Tejeda. Its bars and gardens are open to non-residents, and the restaurant serves local dishes. There are also currency exchange facilities. (At the time of writing, however, there was no accommodation open to visitors). The Canarian style building was designed by the architect Nestor de la Torre. From the patio, on a clear day, a tremendous vista is obtained across the island and the seas to Tenerife and Gomera. Across the road from the *Parador* looking between the pine trees, it is sometimes possible to see Fuerteventura.

Inland route 4

Pinar de Tamadaba — Cuevas de las Cruces: 40 kms; Pinar de Tamadaba — Mogan: 73 kms; Pinar de Tamadaba — San Nicolás de Tolentino

An extended tour by jeep or motorcycle via Artenara and Pinar de Tamadaba from Las Palmas or the south will be a thrilling experience for young holidaymakers. As many of the mountain roads are unmade and have tortuous bends, it is sensible either to travel in the company of an experienced driver or join one of the jeep tours that depart regularly from the main tourist centres: they are all well advertised in the local papers, most hotels and travel agents. Do allow plenty time for the journey as the distance is deceptive.

If you are in a jeep and have a head for heights and a seat for bumpy rides. then it is possible to get from Tamadaba to the west coast by a minor road which goes past three manmade reservoirs, the so-called *presas,* to reach **Hoya de Pineda** — a beautiful but slow ride that leads down the mountains to just north of the **Cuevas de las Cruces** on the C810.

An even more adventurous route from the forest leads to Mogan on the southwest coast. This road is under construction and should only be taken on a fine day in a jeep, as the clouds can come down very quickly. The views are spectacular and well worth the inconvenience, and the silence is magical. We stress that this is a strenuous ride and should only be attempted by the really fit.

Another adventurous route down from the Tamadaba forest is to take the minor road to Acusa and then continue on a track to San Nicolás de Tolentino on the west coast, about thirty kilometres from Artenara. It must be emphasised that this is a route for jeep type vehicles only as it is really steep with hairpin bends down the side of the mountain. In the high ridges you are likely to see buzzards and eagles in slow sweeps searching for their prey. Some cave dwellings and a viewpoint will be passed, otherwise hold on to your seat and enjoy a really wild, hectic journey. In springtime the aroma of the pine trees and wild herbs and shrubs will scent the air. If you can endure the bumpy ride it will be a memorable occasion.

Inland route 5

Cruz de Tejeda — Tejeda — Ayacate — San Bartolomé de Tirajana — Santa Lucia — Temisas — Fataga — Maspalomas: about 37 km

Yet another way to return from the centre of the island, and more manageable for cars, is to turn south at Cruz de Tejeda towards the attractive village of **Tejeda.** Lying at over 914 m, it is pretty and peaceful with many orange and lemon groves. It has a useful petrol station. A twisting road passes craggy mountain peaks, including Benjaiga and Roque Nublo 1817m, in a landscape reminiscent of the surface of the moon. At the village of **Ayacate** a quaint roadside bar is gaining much popularity. There are other roadside bars and two restaurants with a souvenir and craft shop *(artesania)* which make popular stopping places. Between Tejeda and Ayacate are several walks and some Guanche caves that can be visited. Roque Nublo was regarded as sacred by the Guanches, and when one sees this huge impressive basalt outline, for all the world like an altar, it is not hard to understand its significance to a primitive people, who for safety's sake gathered together here in the centre of the island.

This mountain region is full of hidden delights, with banks of wild flowers, such as the bright blue of the anchusa, the yellow codesa, often mixed with wild cineraria, pink, purple and white.

This striking volcanic scenery is found in the centre of the island, where roads are narrow and follow tortuous routes.

Most abundant of all are the pink cheiranthus, the white argyranthemum, the yellow broom *(teline microphylla)* and the large buttercup *(ranunculus cortusifolius)* seen along the road sides. At every bend another beautiful vista comes into view, especially if you have a cloudless day.

The route descends very slowly from the mountains, alongside deep ravines so watch the unguarded sides to the road. Keep a look out for coaches and motorcaravans and be prepared to reverse in narrow places, sometimes with sheer edges! This exciting and pictorial drive will lead to **San Bartolomé de Tirajana,** which is a veritable oasis at the foot of the crags. Palm trees abound and the land is terraced and cultivated, the red-roofed houses well built. It comes as quite a shock to return to civilisation after this drive in the remote and peaceful mountains.

Should you wish for some refreshment after such an exciting drive you can go to the bar restaurant, El Castillo Mirador, just south of San Bartolomé. Meals are served from 0900 hrs, the speciality is Canarian cooking, and the clear air and views are superb.

From San Bartolomé you can join the road to Aguimes, via Santa Lucia and Temisas, a distance of twenty three kilometres —

although the road is winding and narrow and it will seem much further than this — enabling you to rejoin the C812 for the drive back to Las Palmas.

At **Santa Lucia** you are in one of the most attractive of the mountain villages, for many years peaceful and remote. Now it is being developed for tourism. A museum has been created out of an old rambling house and unfortunately it has been faced with volcanic bricks to make a pseudo fort, Fortelezia. However, this museum is extremely interesting to those interested in Guanche memorabilia. Two complete skeletons show just how tall was this primitive race, and display cases of grass skirts, weapons and household implements give an idea of their way of life. Other rooms have archaeological exhibitions, pottery and leather goods. At the side of this museum, up a lane, is the entrance to a large outdoor restaurant, Hao, set amid palm trees. This rustic eating place is popular with the Canarians as well as with coach excursions. It has a children's playground. We hope that the toilet facilities will have improved by the time you visit.

The road south winds its way along the side of the mountains to reach the olive producing village of **Temisas,** which lies below the level of the mountain road. During prehistoric times this was a

South of Arteara a large viewpoint offers extensive views of the inland mountains before the road descends to the coast at Playa del Inglés.

highly populated area. There are still caves, burial grounds and inscriptions to be seen and many archaeological remains have been discovered here. The ravine at Balos, south of Temisas, has examples of drawings of humans and solar symbols in the basalt rocks.

By continuing from Temisas to Aguimes, Ingenio and Carrizal you reach the autopista and head north for Las Palmas. Alternatively, from San Bartolomé visitors who wish to retun to Playa del Inglés or Puerto Rico can take the road via Fataga which leads down a long dry *barranco* to Maspalomas on the south coast. The tiny village of **Fataga** is being developed as a stopping place for coach excursions; several small shops have a selection of island crafts and ceramics for sale. In the bars, samples of local liqueurs are given freely. Try the Ron Miele Indias, a liqueur made of rum and honey; a bottle costs about 400 pesetas (£2.06) and it will taste wonderful after your mountain ride!

One further stop should be made along your route, at a viewpoint just south of **Arteara.** A splendid panorama shows the wondrous red ochre mountains, then the shoreline and modern hotels of Maspalomas, with the great sand dunes and the blue sea beyond.

The noise and bustle of the traffic as you reach Maspalomas contrasts sharply with the tranquillity of central Gran Canaria. Anyone who makes the journey from the north east coast through the Cumbre to the arid south cannot fail to appreciate the aptness of describing the island as 'a continent in miniature' for, small as it is, there seems to be everything: fishing villages, an international port, old churches, green valleys, silent forests, ancient caves, craggy mountains, majestic peaks, historic sites, and a desert-like zone. Together with modern comforts, entertainment and sports, and sea, sand and sunshine, these must put Gran Canaria very high on the list of beautiful islands.

Finale

Isla de Contraste is how the people of Gran Canaria describe their island, and visitors too, need not look very far to realise that this is indeed an apt description.

Along the southern shores you will find a myriad of entertainments, hotels, apartments, warm seas and wonderful golden beaches. Las Palmas, the great city which links the sea roads from Europe, Africa and the Americas, hums with colourful life. Full of history and modern culture, it also has large departmental stores and a host of small bazaars. At night the streets are a-glitter with the sleazy and the sophisticated.

Inland mighty mountains beckon, their great landscapes varying from rugged, rocky peaks full of ancient Guanche hideaway caves, to gentle valleys of orange groves and almond blossom, the clear air fragrant with their perfume.

All this, and more, is here, the delight of being in Gran Canaria.

Mary stops to check the route through the Pinar de Tamadaba.

Spanish/English Vocabulary

Public signs and notices

abierto	open
aseo	toilet
caballeros	gentlemen
cerrado	closed
empuje	push
entrada	entrance
libre	free/vacant
muelle	quay
ocupado	engaged
privado	private
salida	depart/way out
senoras	ladies
se alquilar	to rent
se prohibe	forbidden
servicio	toilet
se vende	for sale
se prohibe estacioner	no parking
se prohibe fumar	no smoking
tire	pull

Drinks

beer	*cerveza*
coffee/black	*café solo*
Coffee/white	*café con leche*
gin	*ginebra*
ice	*hielo*
sherry	*jerez*
squash	*zumo*
tea	*té*
water	*agua*
wine dry	*vino seco*
red	*vino tinto*
sweet	*vino dulce*
white	*vino blanco*

Shops and places

bakery	*panaderia*
butcher's shop	*carnicería*
cake shop	*pastelería*
chemist	*farmacia*
church	*iglesia*
cinema	*cine*
dairy	*lecheria*
fishmonger	*pescadería*
grocer	*alimentacion*
ironmonger	*ferreteria*
library	*biblioteca*
market	*mercado*
post office	*correos*
shoe shop	*zapatería*
stationer	*papeleria*
theatre	*teatro*
town hall	*ayuntamiento*
view point	*mirador*

Restaurant

Bill	*cuenta*
bottle	*botella*
breakfast	*desayuno*
cup	*taza*
dinner	*cena*
drink	*bebida*
fork	*tenedor*
glass	*vaso*
knife	*cuchillo*
lunch	*almuerzo*
plate	*plato*
sandwich	*bocadillo*
spoon	*cuchara*
table	*mesa*
tip	*propina*
waiter	*camarero*

Useful words

all	*todo*
before	*antes*
behind	*detras*
big	*grande*
cold	*frio*
everybody	*todos*
fast	*rapido*
food	*alimento*
good	*bueno*
here	*aqui*
high	*alto*
hot	*caliente*
how many?	*cuantos*
how much?	*cuanto*
left (direction)	*izquierda*
like	*como*
little (quantity)	*poco*
lost	perdido
many	*mas*
near	*cerca*
no	*no*
old	*viejo*
please	*por favor*
right (direction)	*derecha*
slow	*lento*
Soon	*pronto*
thank you	*gracias*
too many	*demasiados*
too much	*demasiado*
under	*debajo*
up	*arriba*
very	*muy*
well	*bien*
when?	*cuando*
why?	*por que*
without	*sin*
with	*con*
yes	*si*

Days of the week

Sunday	*Domingo*
Monday	*Lunes*
Tuesday	*Martes*
Wednesday	*Miercoles*
Thursday	*Jueves*
Friday	*Viernes*
Saturday	*Sabado*

Months

January	*Enero*
February	*Febrero*
March	*Marzo*
April	*Abril*
May	*Mayo*
June	*Junio*
July	*Julio*
August	*Agosto*
September	*Septiembre*
October	*Octubre*
November	*Noviembre*
December	*Diciembre*

Numbers

one	*uno, una*
two	*dos*
three	*tres*
four	*cuatro*
five	*cinco*
six	*seis*
seven	*siete*
eight	*ocho*
nine	*nueve*
ten	*diez*

Food

apple	*manzana*	mushrooms	*setas*
banana	*platano*	mussels	*mejillónes*
beef	*vaca*	mustard	*mostaza*
biscuit	*galleta*	oil	*aceite*
bread	*pan*	olives	*aceitunas*
butter	*mantequilla*	onions	*cebollas*
cabbage	*col*	orange	*naranja*
caramel			
pudding	*flan*	peach	melocoton
carrots	*zanahorias*	pear	*pera*
cauliflower	*coliflor*	peas	*guisantes*
cheese	*queso*	pepper	*pimienta*
chicken	*pollo*	pork	*cerda*
chop	*chuleta*	potatoes	*patatas*
cream	*nata*	rice	*arroz*
cucumber	*pepino*	salad	*ensalada*
egg	*huevo*	salt	*sal*
fish	*pescado*	sauce	*salsa*
french beans	*judias verde*	sausages	*chorizo*
grapes	*uvas*	shrimps	*gambas*
ham	*jamón*	strawberries	*fresas*
ice cream	*helados*	sugar	*azucar*
lamb	*cordero*	toast	*tostado*
lemon	*limon*	veal	*ternara*
lobster	*langosta*	vegetables	*verduras*
marmalade	*mermelada*	vinegar	*vinagre*

Appendix B
Wind Force: The Beaufort Scale*

B'Fort No.	Wind Descrip.	Effect on land	Effect on sea	Wind Speed knots	mph	kph	Wave height (m)†
0	Calm	Smoke rises vertically	Sea like a mirror	less than 1			-
1	Light air	Direction shown by smoke but not by wind vane	Ripples with appearance of scales; no foam crests	1-3	1-3	1-2	-
2	Light breeze	Wind felt on face; leaves rustle; wind vanes move	Small wavelets; crests do not break	4-6	4-7	6-11	0.15-0.30
3	Gentle breeze	Leaves and twigs in motion wind extends light flag	Large wavelets; crests begin to break; scattered white horses	7-10	8-12	13-19	0.60-1.00
4	Moderate breeze	Small branches move; dust and loose paper raised	Small waves, becoming longer; fairly frequent white horses	11-16	13-18	21-29	1.00-1.50
5	Fresh breeze	Small trees in leaf begin to sway	Moderate waves; many white horses; chance of some spray	17-21	19-24	30-38	1.80-2.50
6	Strong breeze	Large branches in motion; telegraph wires whistle	Large waves begin to form; white crests extensive; some spray	22-27	25-31	40-50	3.00-4.00

	Name	Land description	Sea description				
7	Near gale	Whole trees in motion; difficult to walk against wind	Sea heaps up; white foam from breaking waves begins to be blown in streaks	28-33	32-38	51-61	4.00-6.00
8	Gale	Twigs break off trees; progress impeded	Moderately high waves; foam blown in well-marked streaks	34-40	39-46	63-74	5.50-7.50
9	Strong gale	Chimney pots and slates blown off	High waves; dense streaks of foam; wave crests begin to roll over; heavy spray	41-47	47-54	75-86	7.00-9.75
10	Storm	Trees uprooted; considerable structural damage	Very high waves, overhanging crests; dense white foam streaks; sea takes on white appearance; visibility affected	48-56	66-63	88-100	9.00-12.50
11	Violent storm	Widespread damage, seldom experienced in England	Exceptionally high waves; dense patches of foam; wave crests blown into froth; visibility affected	57-65	64-75	101-110	11.30-16.00
12	Hurricane	Winds of this force encountered only in Tropics	Air filled with foam & spray; visibility seriously affected	65 +	75 +	120 +	13.70 +

* Introduced in 1805 by Sir Francis Beaufort (1774-1857) hydrographer to the Navy

+ First figure indicates average height of waves; second figure indicates maximum height.

APPENDIX C: USEFUL CONVERSION TABLES

Distance/Height

feet	ft or m	metres
3.281	1	0.305
6.562	2	0.610
9.843	3	0.914
13.123	4	1.219
16.404	5	1.524
19.685	6	8.829
22.966	7	2.134
26.247	8	2.438
29.528	9	2.743
32.808	10	3.048
65.617	20	8.096
82.081	25	7.620
164.05	50	15.25
328.1	100	30.5
3281.	1000	305.

Weight

pounds	kg or lb	kilograms
2.205	1	0.454
4.409	2	0.907
8.819	4	1.814
13.228	6	2.722
17.637	8	3.629
22.046	10	4.536
44.093	20	9.072
55.116	25	11.340
110.231	50	22.680
220.462	100	45.359

Distance

miles	**km or mls**	kilometres
0.621	1	1.609
1.243	2	3.219
1.864	3	4.828
2.486	4	6.437
3.107	5	8.047
3.728	6	9.656
4.350	7	11.265
4.971	8	12.875
5.592	9	14.484
6.214	10	16.093
12.428	20	32.186
15.534	25	40.234
31.069	50	80.467
62.13	100	160.93
621.3	1000	1609.3

Dress sizes

Size	bust/hip inches	bust/hip centimetres
8	30/32	76/81
10	32/34	81/86
12	34/36	86/91
14	36/38	91/97
16	38/40	97/102
18	40/42	102/107
20	42/44	107/112
22	44/46	112/117
24	46/48	117/122

Tyre pressure

lb per sq in	kg per sq cm
14	0.984
16	1.125
18	1.266
20	1.406
22	1.547
24	1.687
26	1.828
28	1.969
30	2.109
40	2.812

Temperature

centigrade	fahrenheit
0	32
5	41
10	50
20	68
30	86
40	104
50	122
60	140
70	158
80	176
90	194
100	212

Oven temperatures

Electric	Gas mark	Centigrade
225	¼	110
250	½	130
275	1	140
300	2	150
325	3	170
350	4	180
375	5	190
400	6	200
425	7	220
450	8	230

Your weight in kilos

stones

kilograms

Liquids

gallons	**gal or l**	litres
0.220	1	4.546
0.440	2	9.092
0.880	4	18.184
1.320	6	27.276
1.760	8	36.368
2.200	10	45.460
4.400	20	90.919
5.500	25	113.649
10.999	50	227.298
21.998	100	454.596

Some handy equivalents for self caterers

1 oz	25 g	1 fluid ounce	25 ml
4 oz	125 g	¼ pt. (1 gill)	142 ml
8 oz	250 g	½ pt.	284 ml
1 lb	500 g	¾ pt.	426 ml
2.2 lb	1 kilo	1 pt.	568 ml
		1¾ pints	1 litre

APPENDIX D: BIBLIOGRAPHY

Abraham, Luis Ortega *First Encounter with the Canary Islands,* 1987. ISBN 84 505 5839 5.

Bramwell, David and Zoë *Wild Flowers of the Canary Islands,* 1984. Stanley Thornes, Cheltenham. ISBN 0 85950 227 9.

Concepción, José Luis *The Guanche Survivors,* 1st Edition 1982. Imprenta Benerga, La Laguna, Tenerife. ISBN 84 398 2173 5.

Lopez Herrera, Salvador *The Canary Islands Through History,* 1978. Graficas Tenerife SA, Santa Cruz de Tenerife. ISBN 84 400 7405 3.

Mason, John and Ann *The Canary Islands,* 1976. Batsford London.

Moeller, Hubert *The Flora of the Canary Islands,* 1981. Republished by Fred Kolbe, Puerto de la Cruz, Tenerife.

Moreno, José Manuel *Guia de las Aves de Las Islas Canarias,* 1988. Editorial Interinsular Canaria SA, Tenerife. ISBN 84 86733 05 7.

Myhill, Henry *The Canary Islands,* 1968. Faber and Faber, London.

Rochford, Noel *Landscapes of Gran Canaria,* 1986. Sunflower Books, London. ISBN 0 948513 03 9.